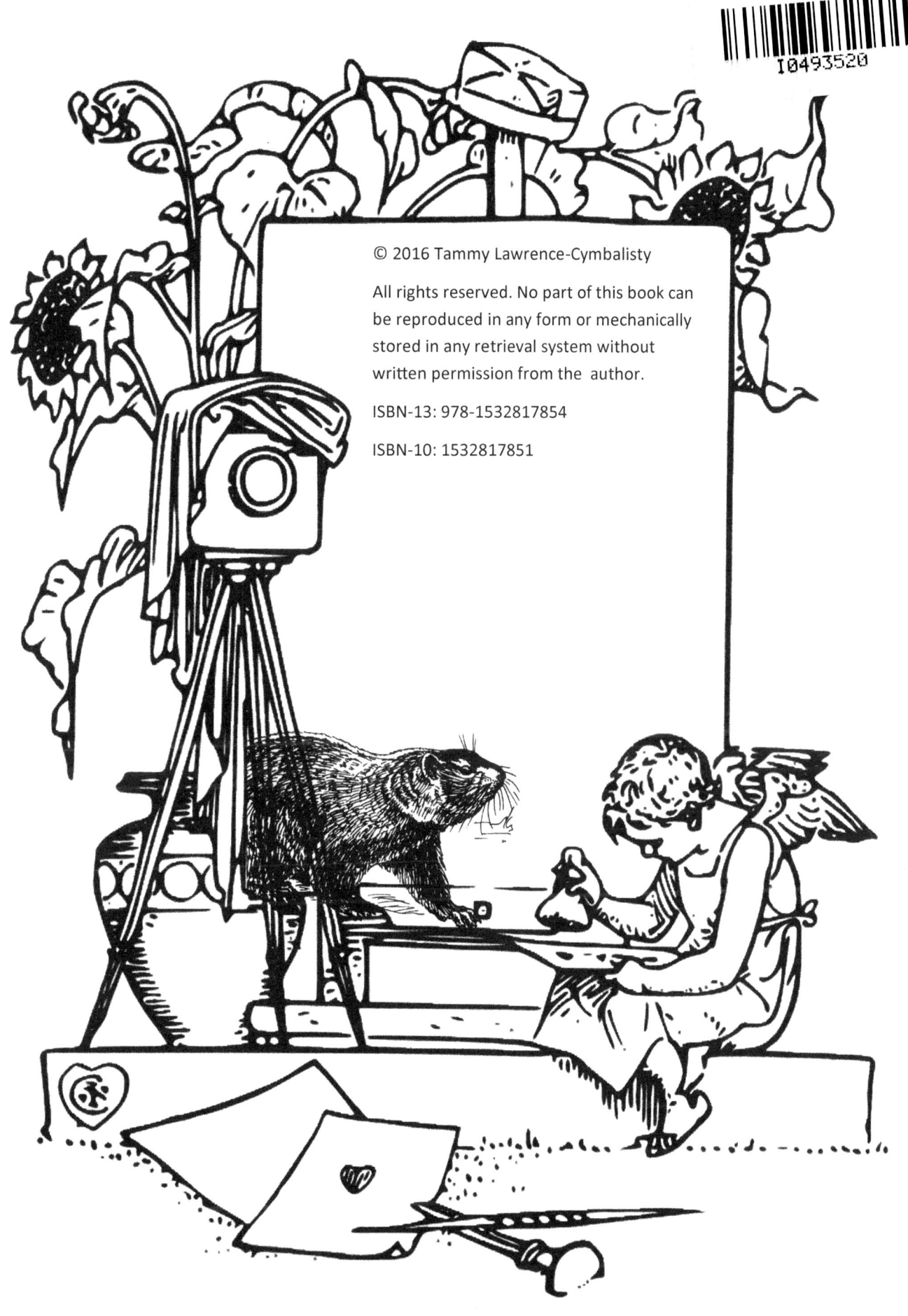

ISBN-13: 978-1532817854

ISBN-10: 1532817851

Welcome to the My Otter Totem Colouring book! Thank you so much for your purchase.

I want to share with you what brought this series of colouring books to fruition. I was doing some re-search on what my next project should be and stumbled across an owl to colour (I have Owl as my totem). I thought about creating a colouring book. I asked the universe, "Should I be focusing on this?" I put the question out there, let it go and left for work. Within two blocks of the house I noticed a billboard with the words "In The Dark; an upcoming exhibit at a museum in Waterloo, Ontario. I laughed when I saw it. Staring back at me from the bulletin board were a huge set of Owl eyes! "Maybe that's a message?" I kept going on my path not giving it much more thought.

I arrived at work ten minutes later to see a tiny envelope on the floor where I normally place my yoga mat (I'm grateful to be a Yoga Teacher) with my name on the front of it. I open it up to find a tiny pewter Owl with the words "Give a Hoot" inscribed on the back! I burst out laughing and shared the story with Wendy; the woman who had gifted me. That decided it there and then!

After I completed the Owl Totem colouring book I thought why stop there? All of the animals of the Zodiac should be represented. As my parents and my Sister-in-law have Wolf as their totems, and being it was close to their birthdays, I thought let's do Wolves! Similar things started to happen; for example I walked into a store just after I made the decision to see a large Wolf microfiber blanket in front of me.

Otter n the Native American Lore is for those born between Jan. 20th—Feb. 18th. Otters are playful, un-conventional and imaginative. The Otter is a good friend, is sensitive, creative and honest. You can find out more about the Native American Lore by searching "Native American Zodiac signs" to see which ani-mal you are.

Whether the Otter is your totem or you simply adore this playful being I hope you enjoy it. Go grab your markers, pens, pencil crayons or paints and your creative juices!

I would suggest placing a piece of paper (you could also choose waxed paper) behind the pictures particu-larly if you are choosing wet mediums to prevent any bleed-through. The pictures have a page between them to help with this additionally. However if you, like me, enjoy using acrylics or watercolour you may need the additional support for the page.

You'll find lots of areas in the pictures to add additional creations. For example you could turn it into a journal by writing about your day in the blank areas, play with some interesting fonts or add your favourite affirmations. You are the artist here so whatever you create will be perfect!

Happy colouring!

Wishing you many continued blessings,

Tammy

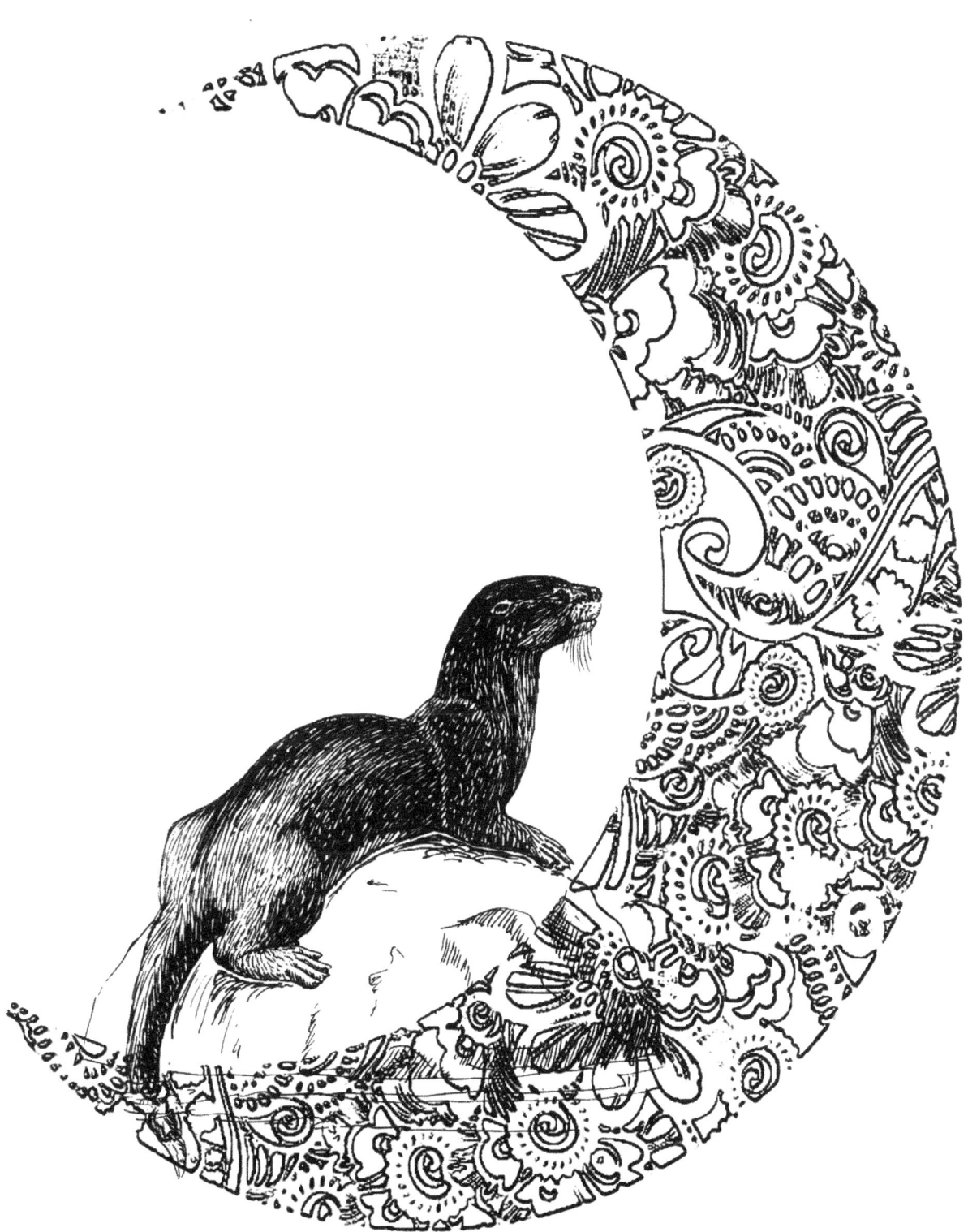

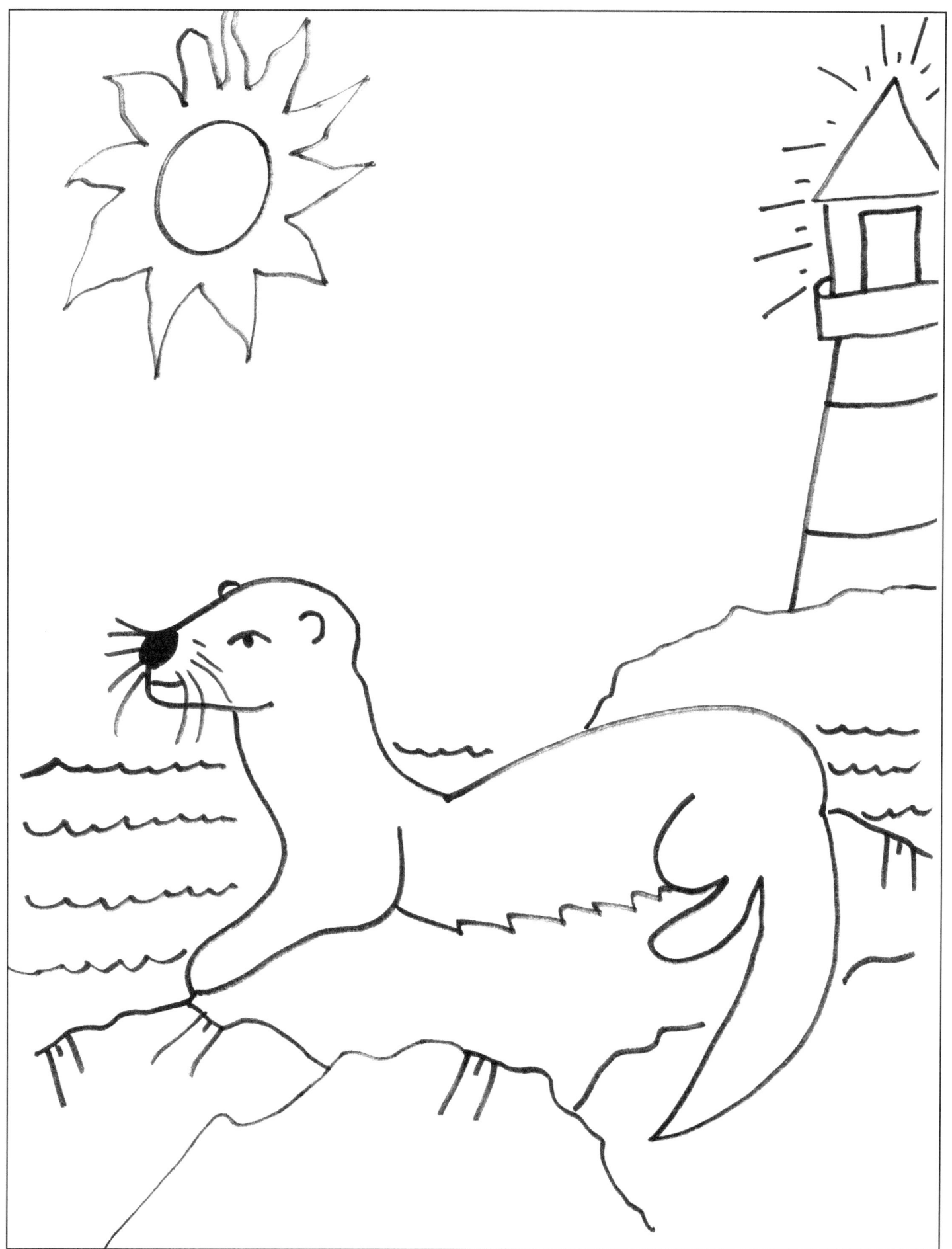

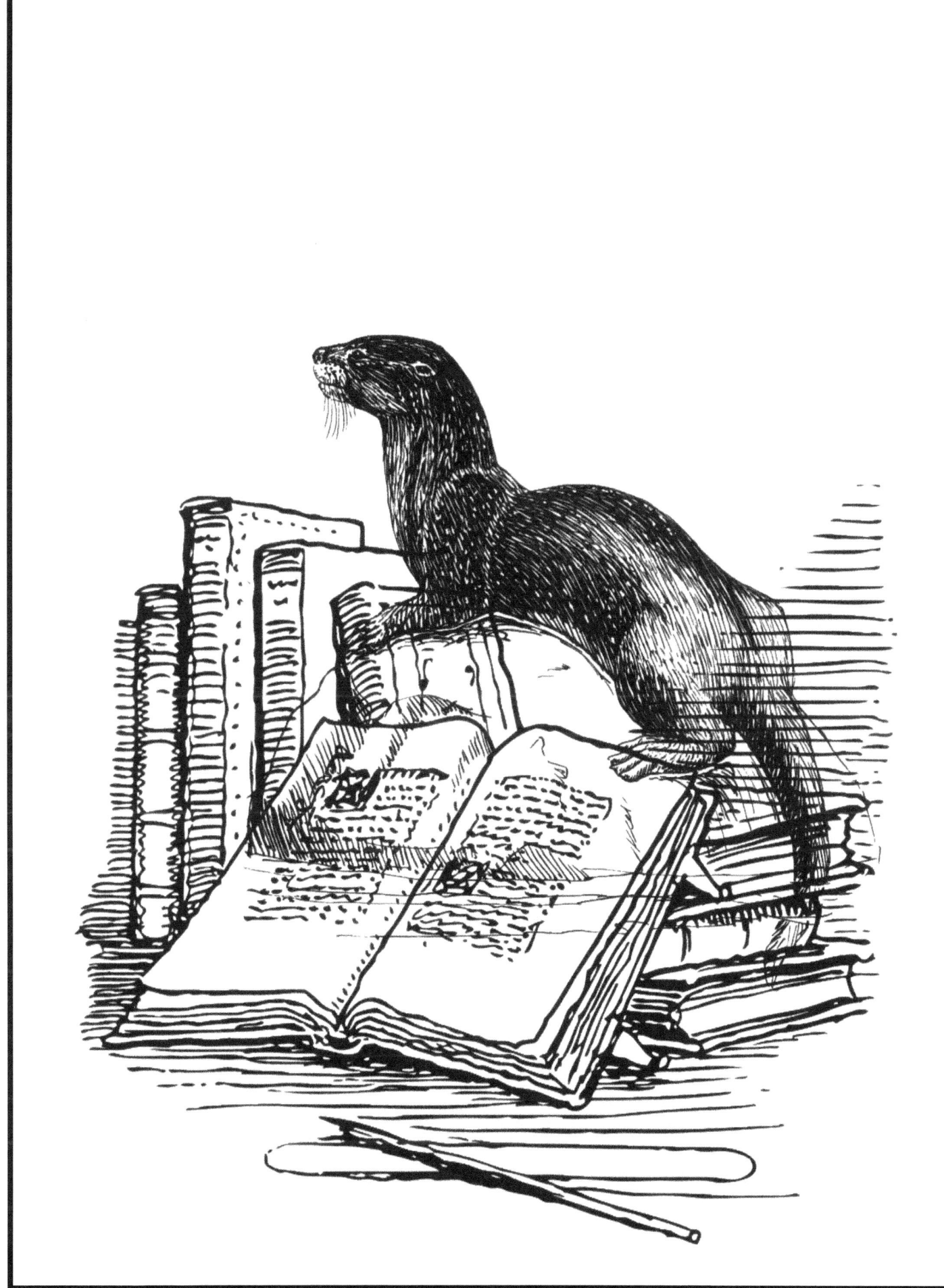

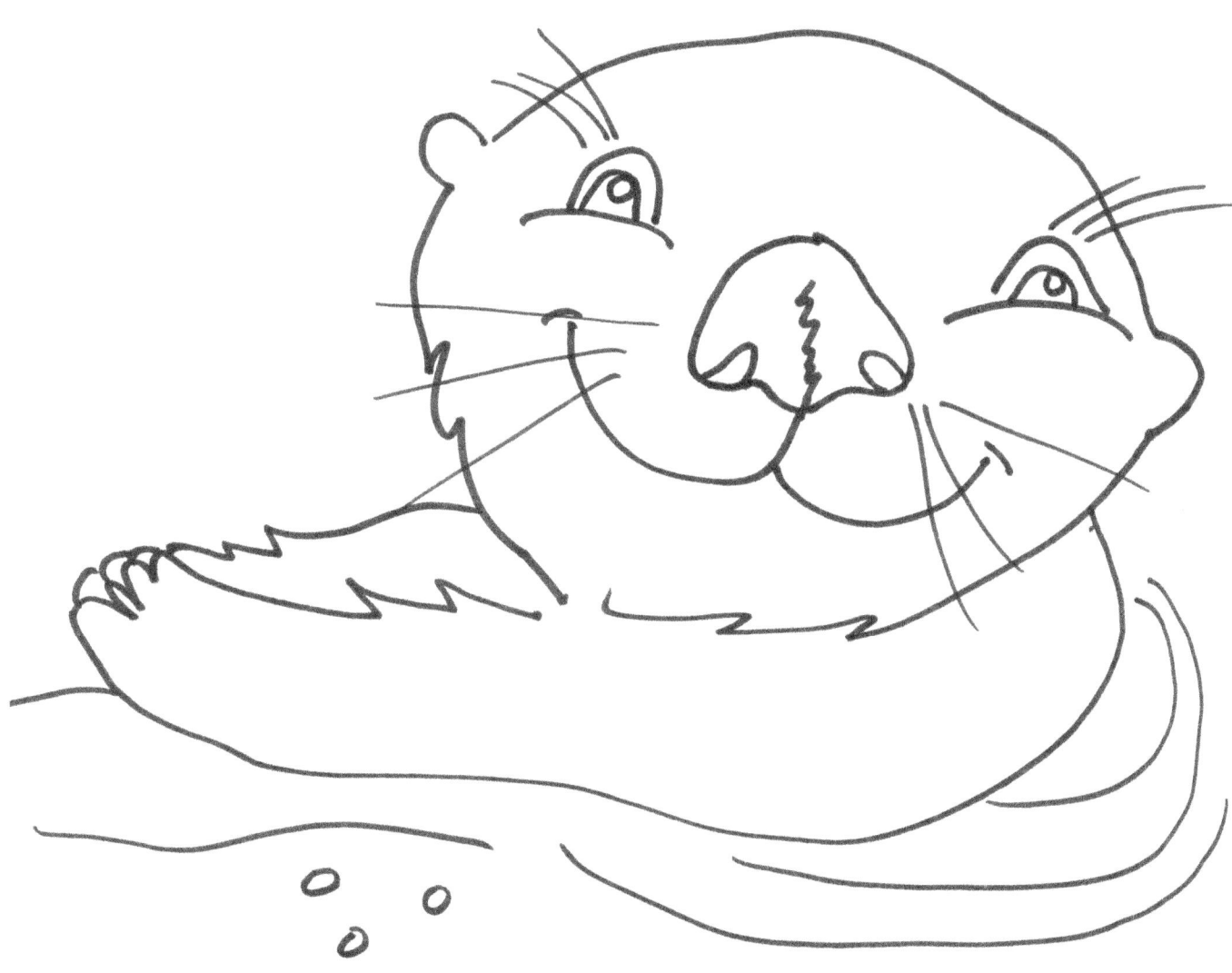

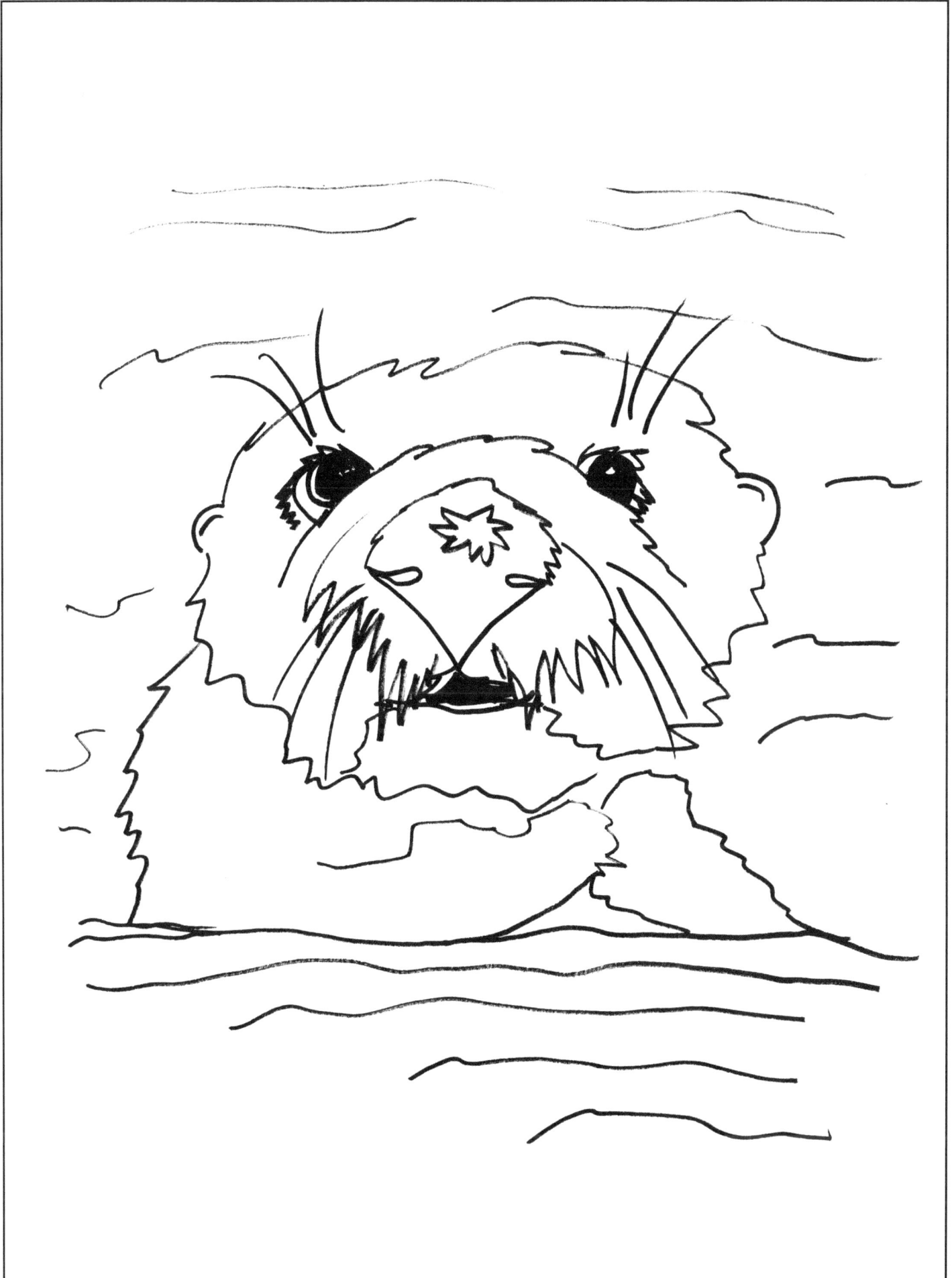

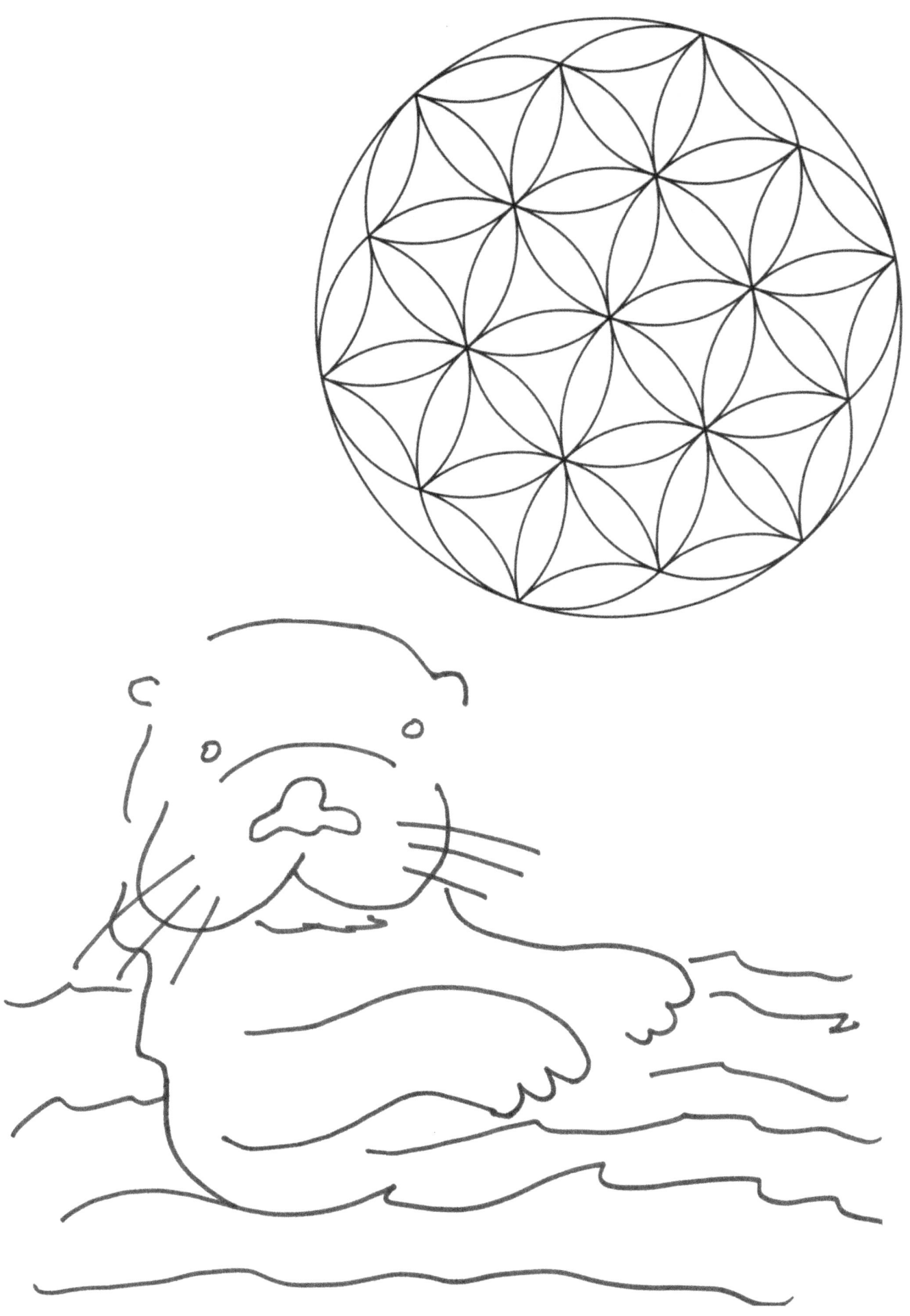

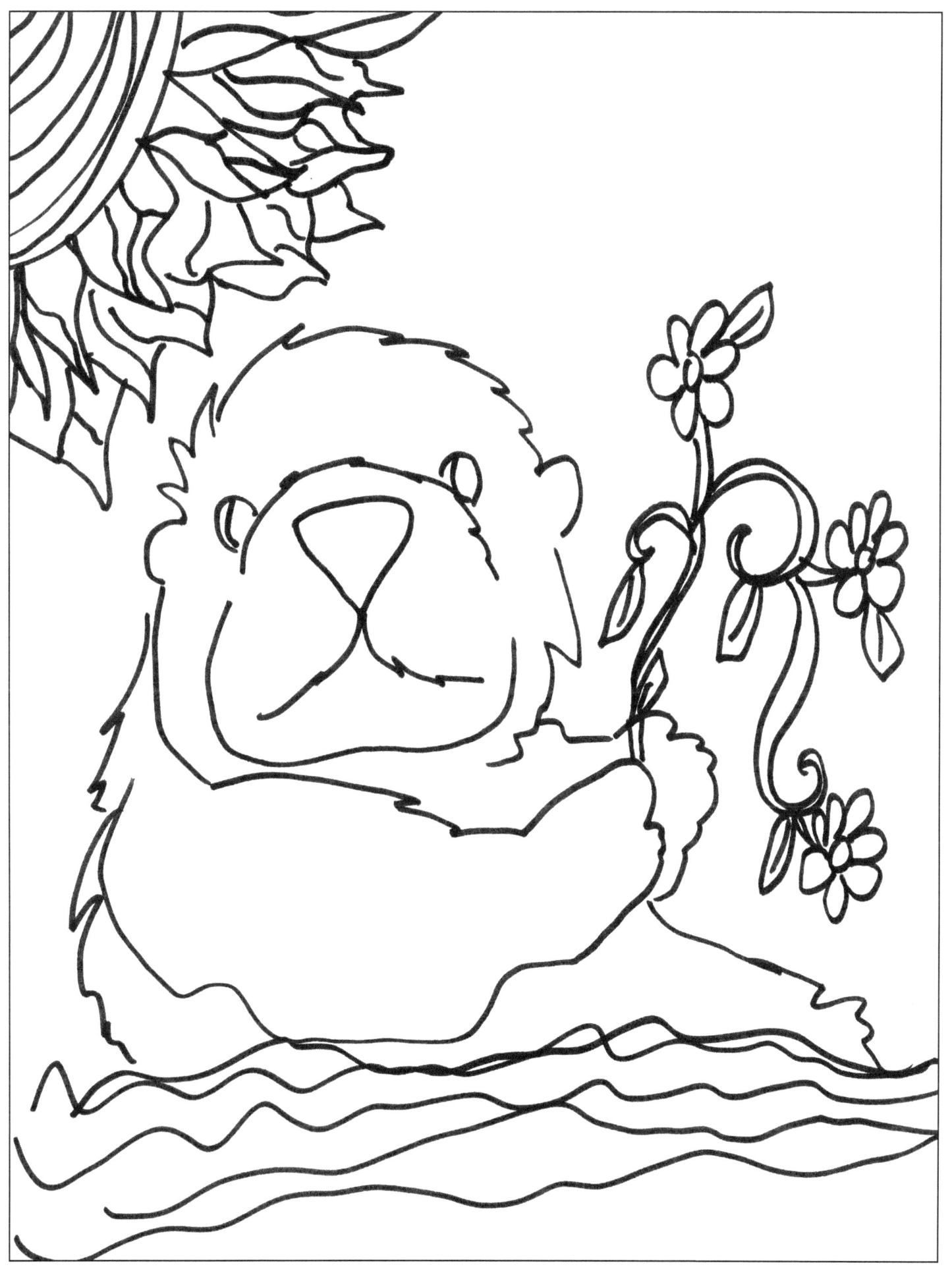

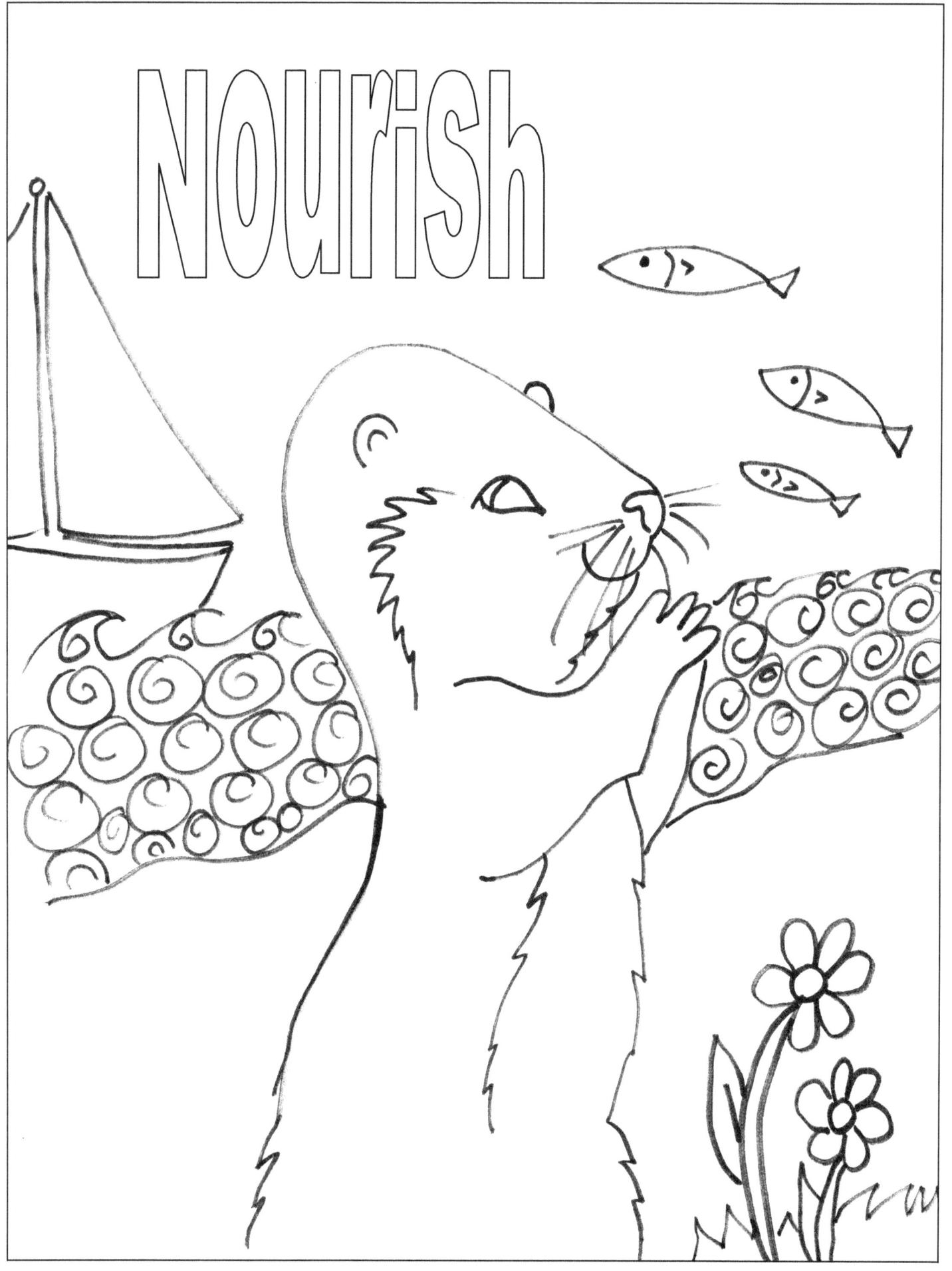

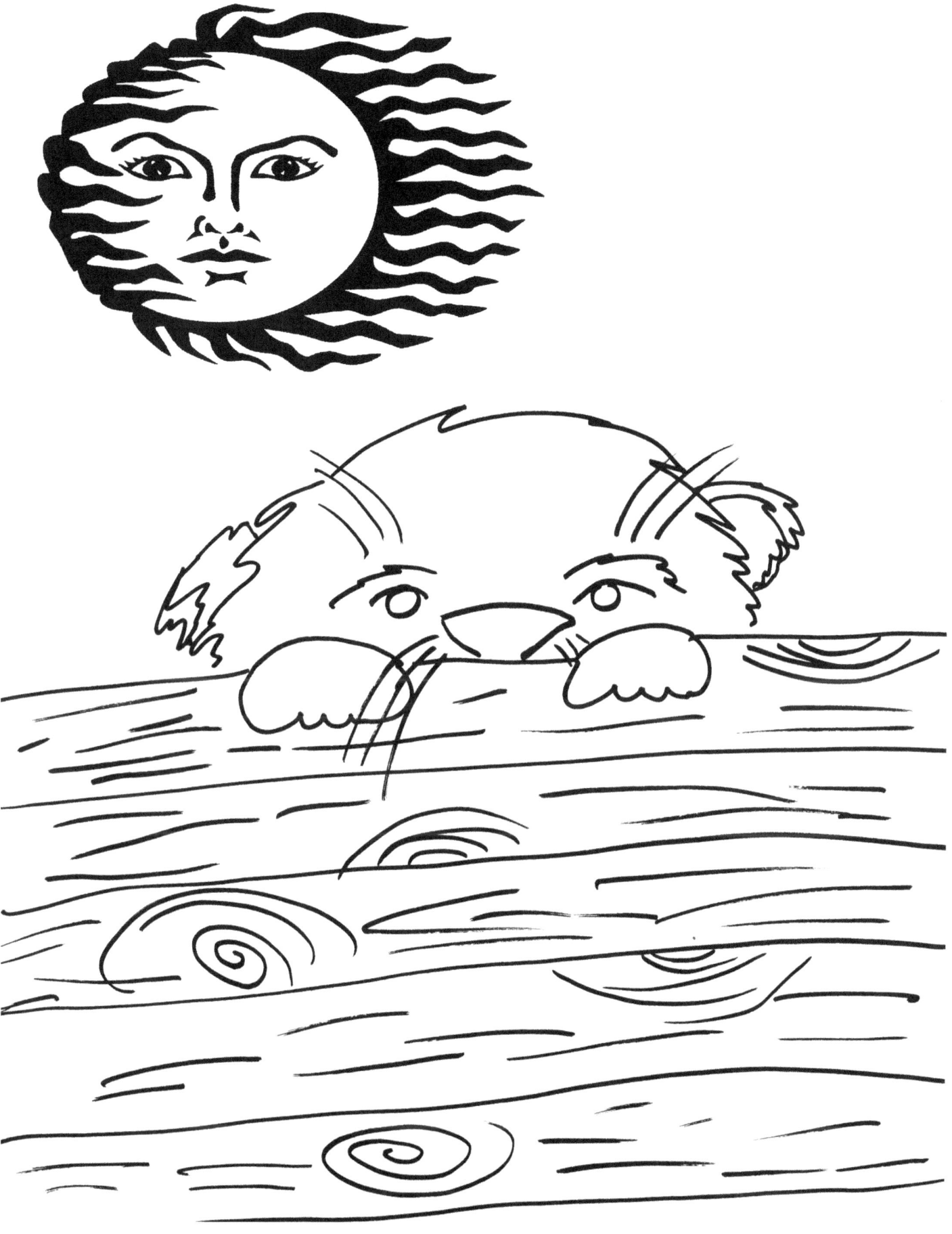

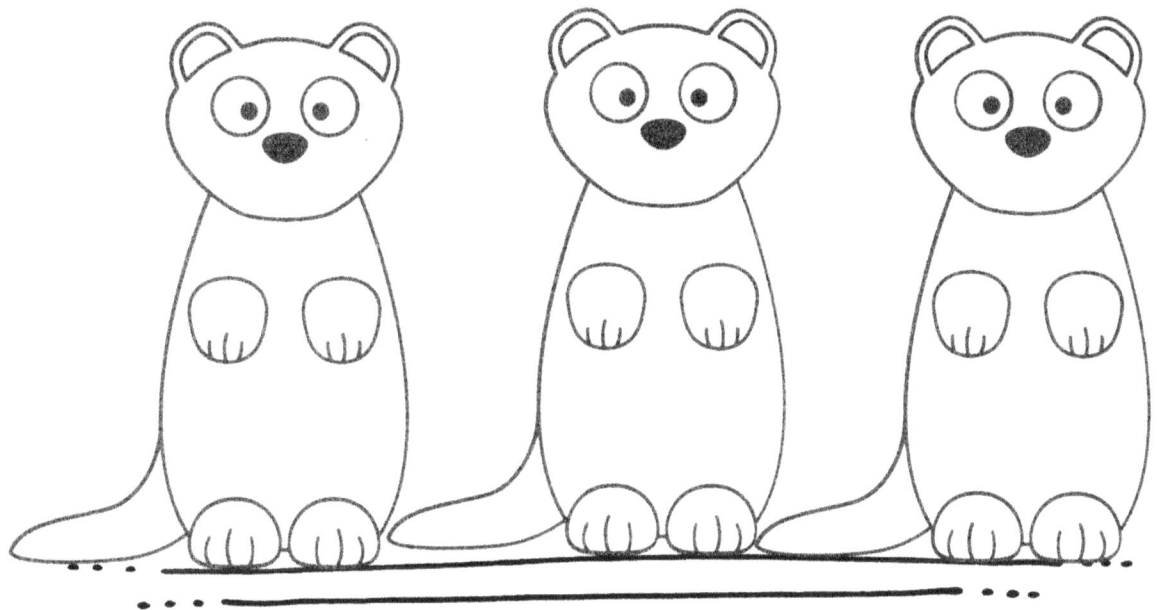

To LIVE with Gratitudes →→→ forever IN my heart

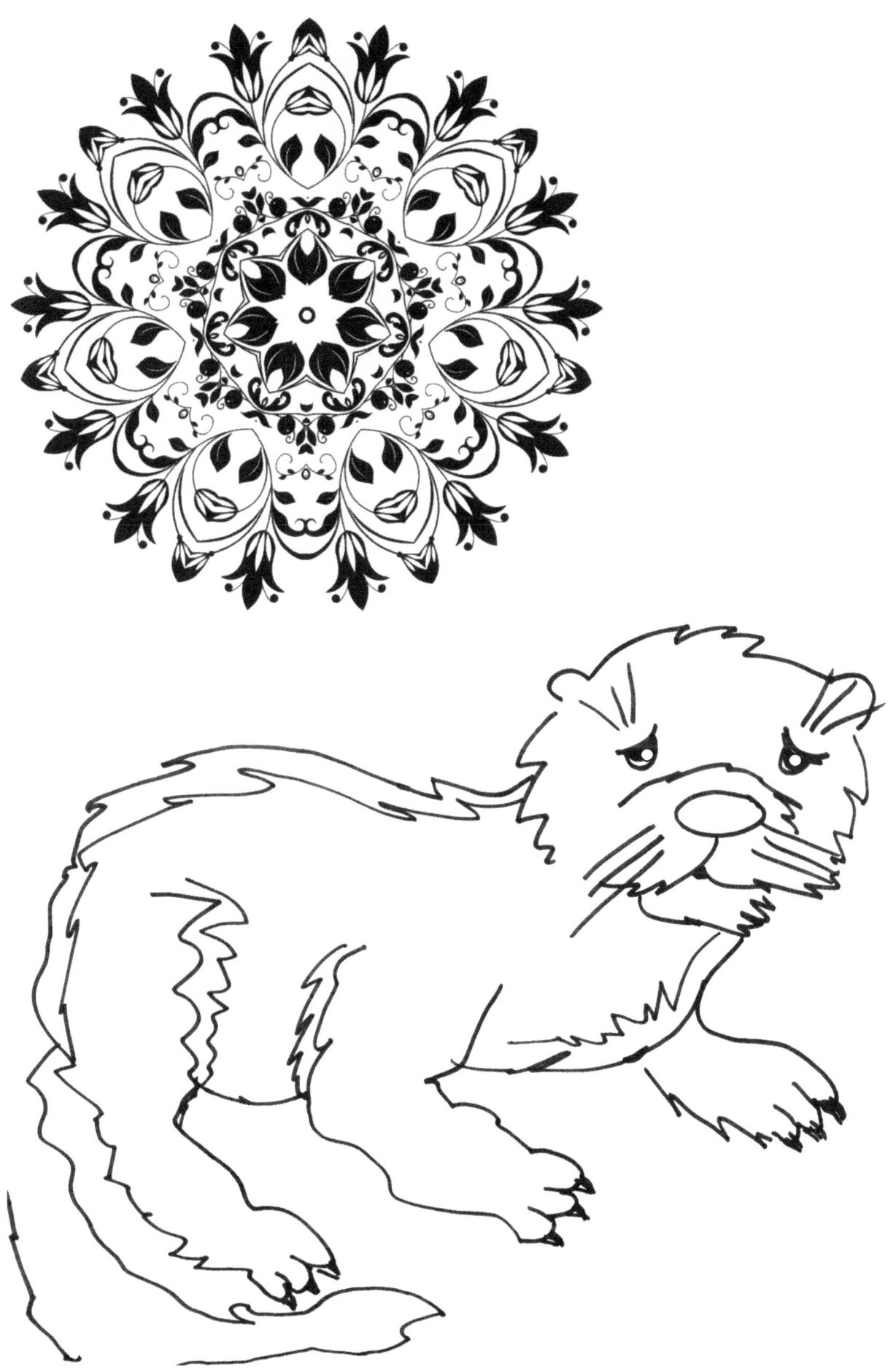

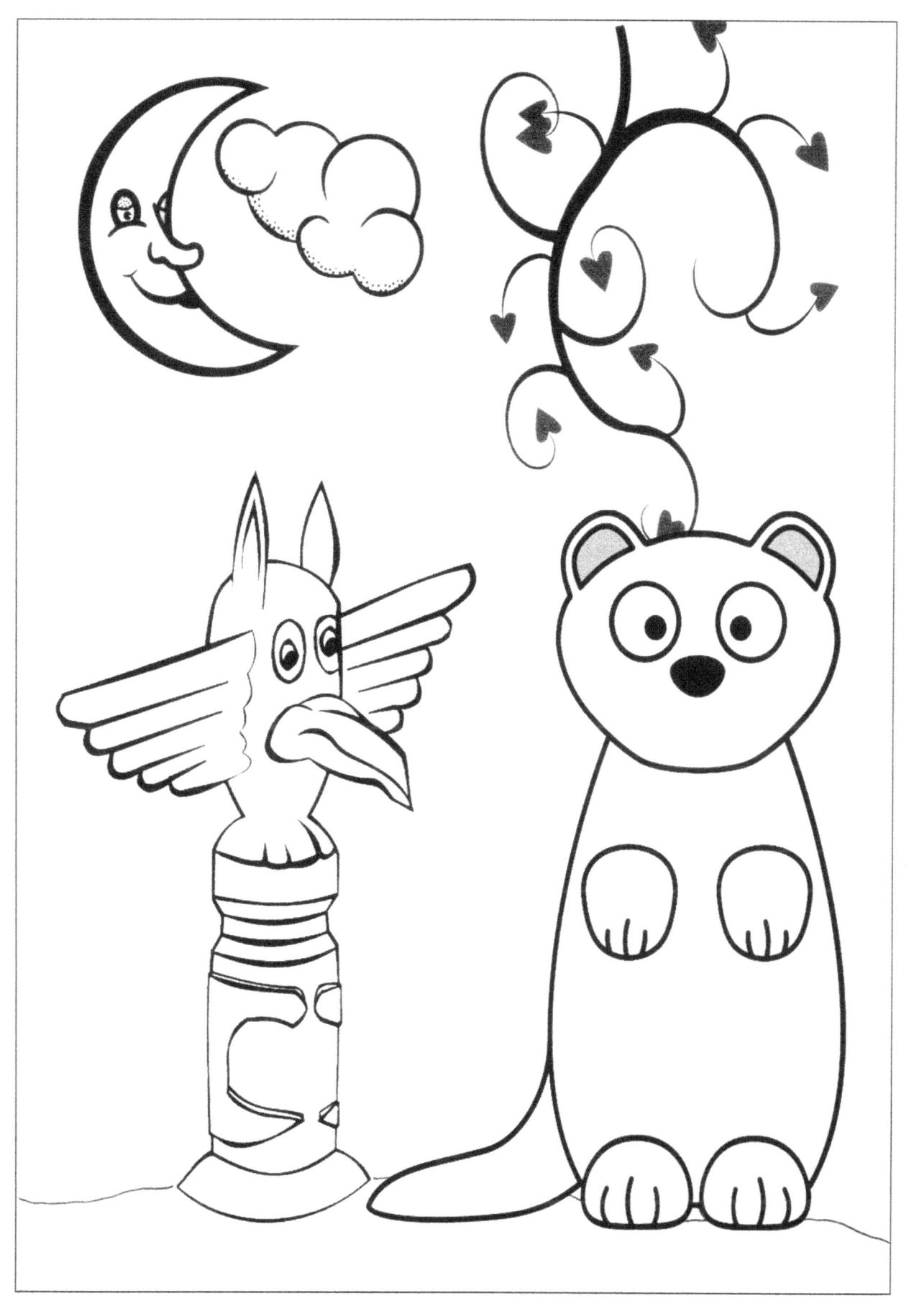

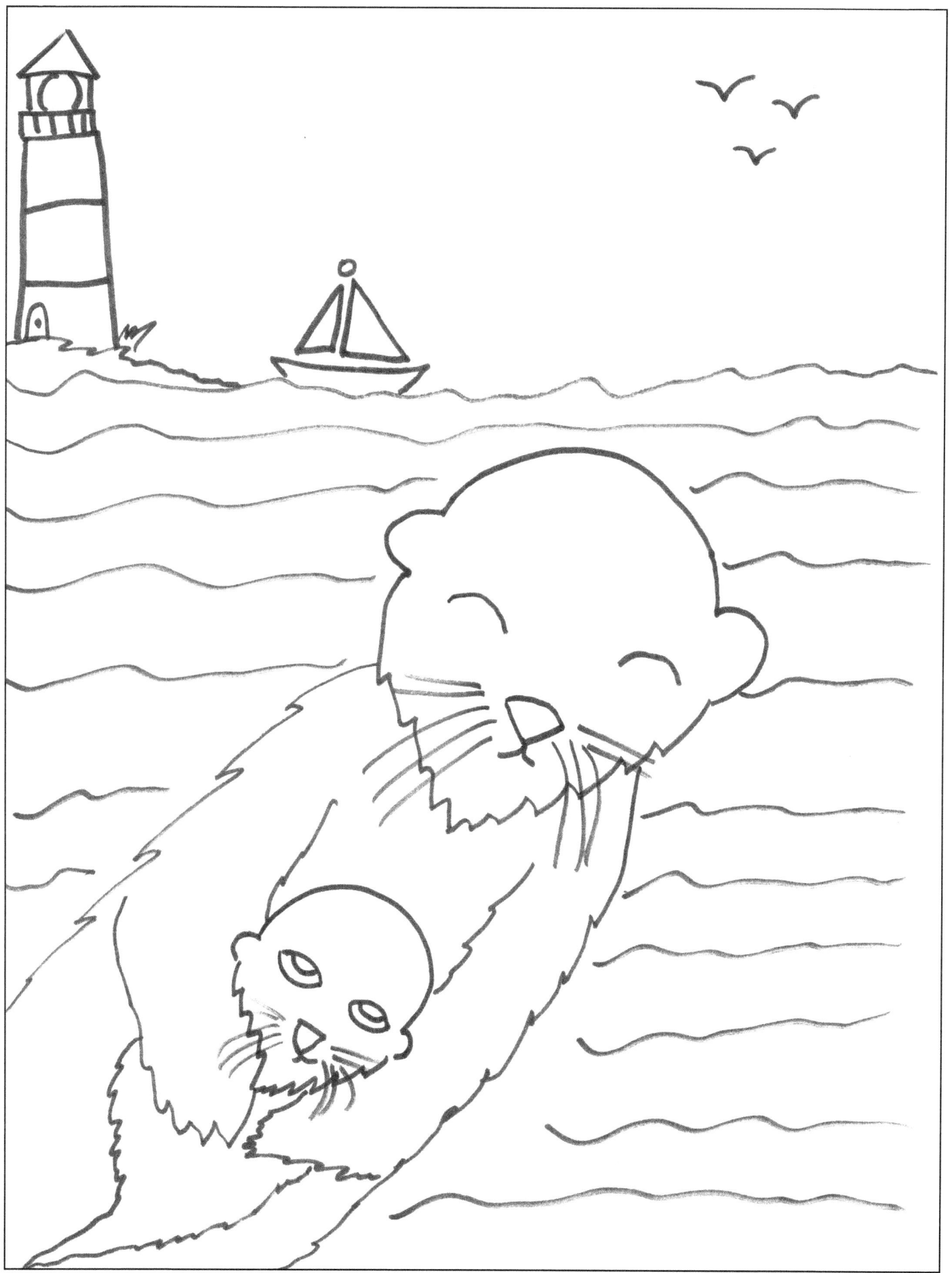

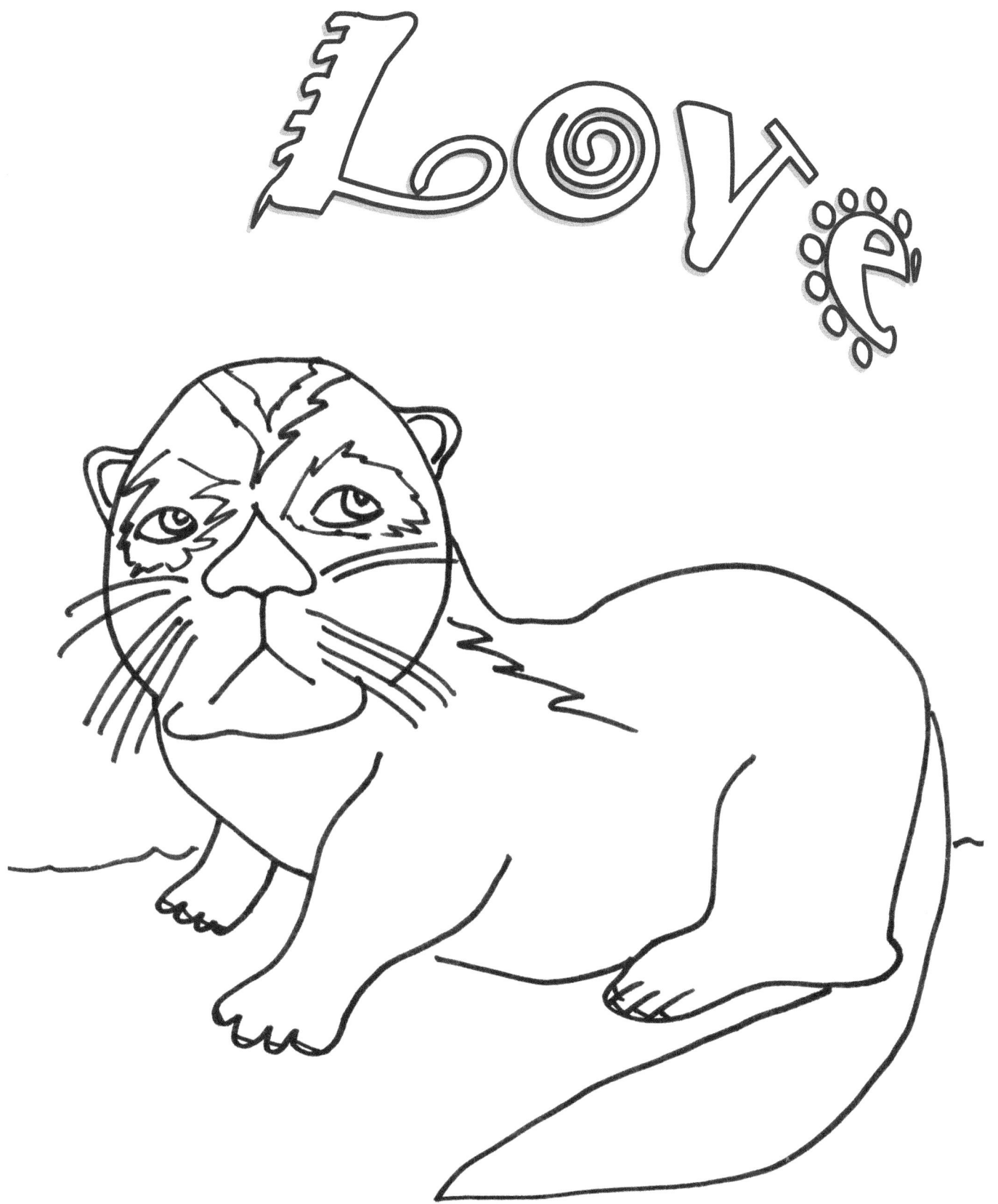

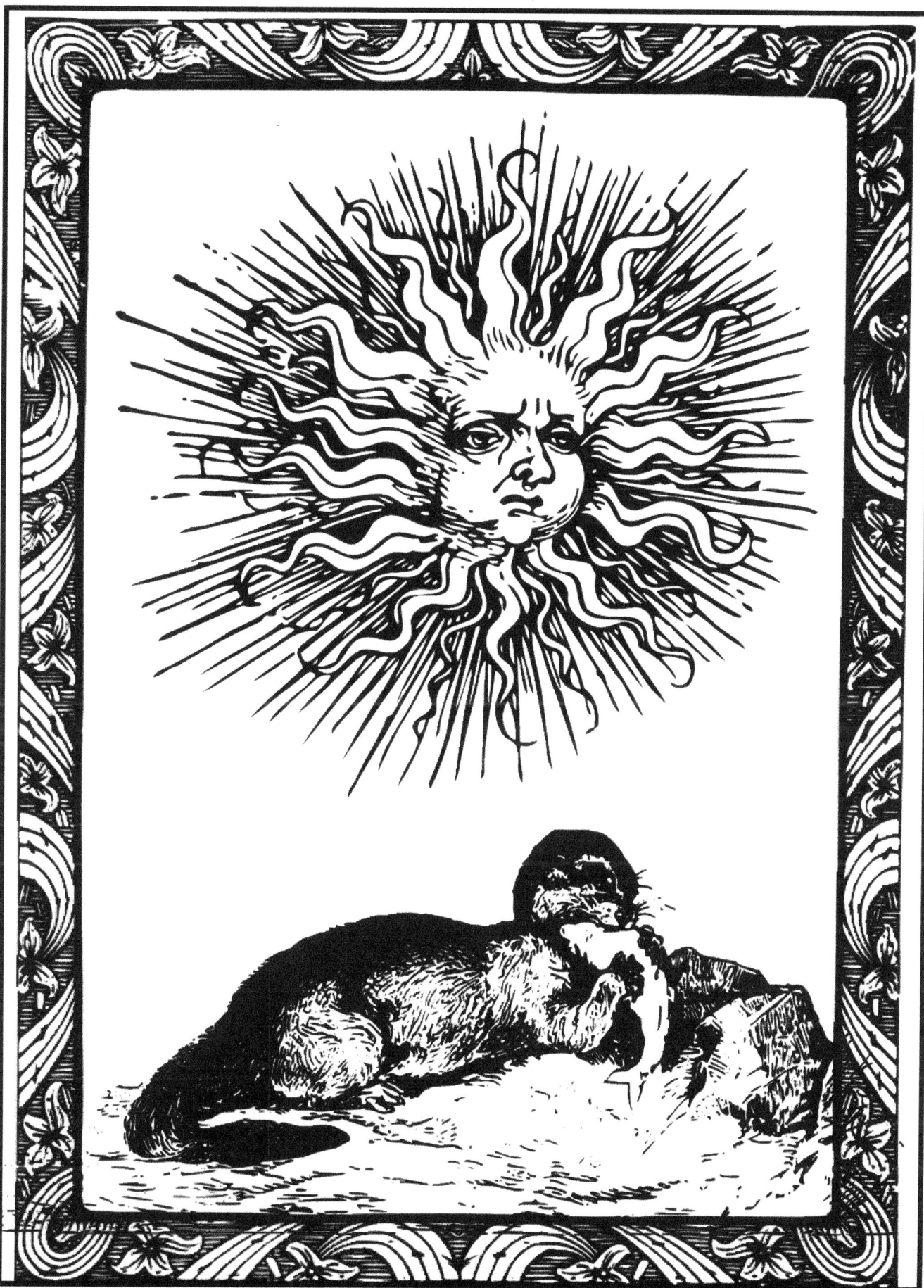

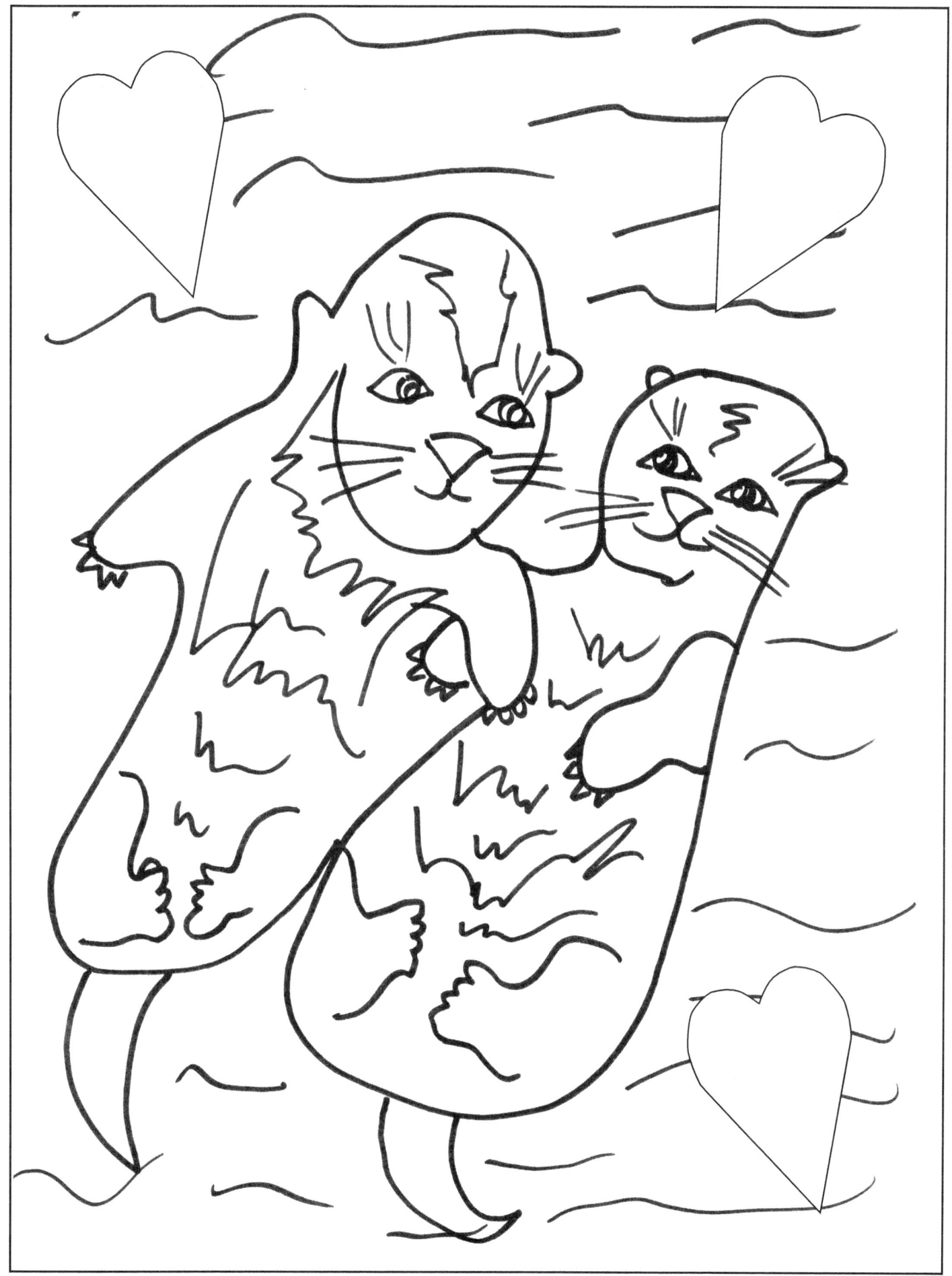

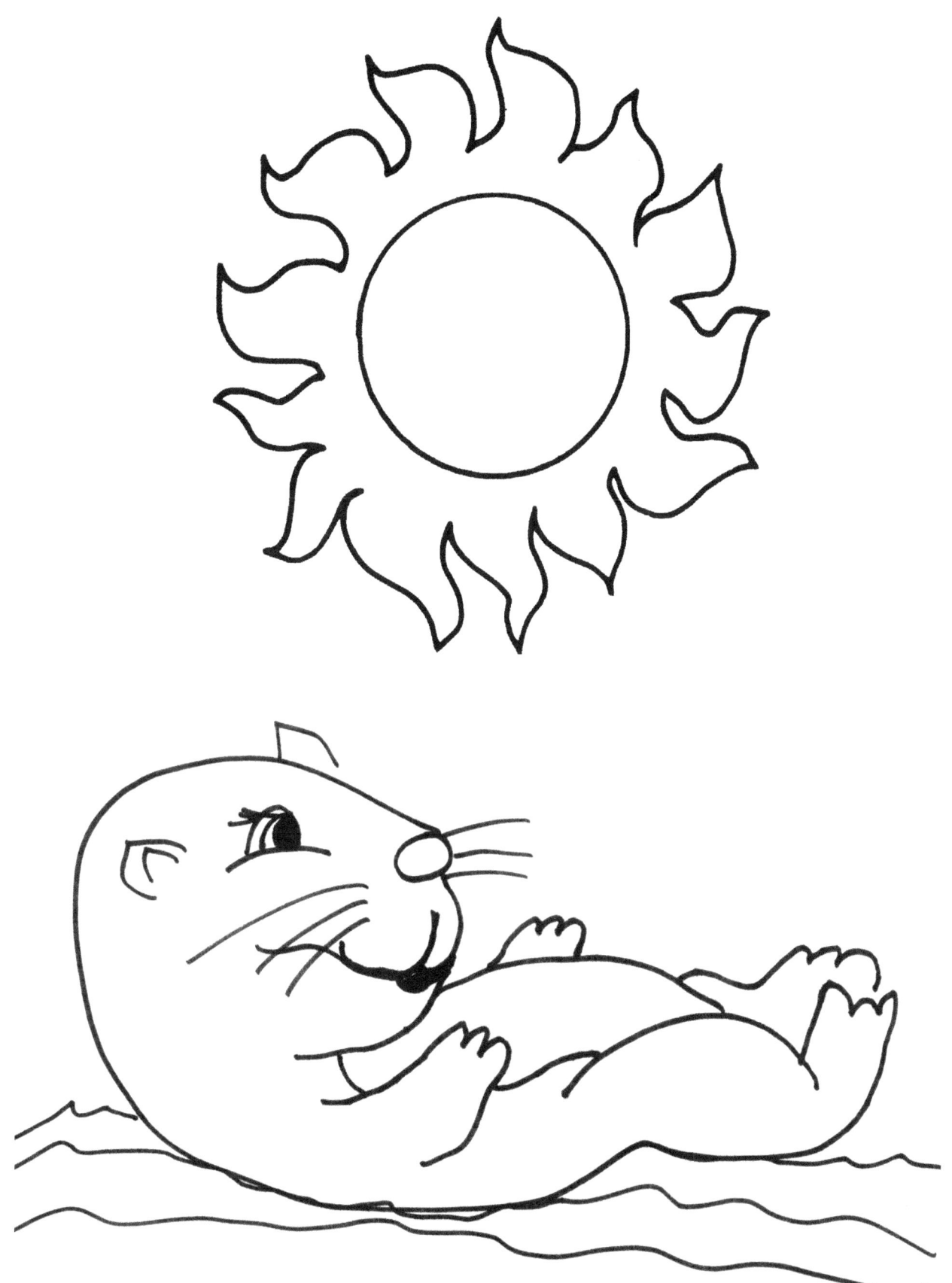

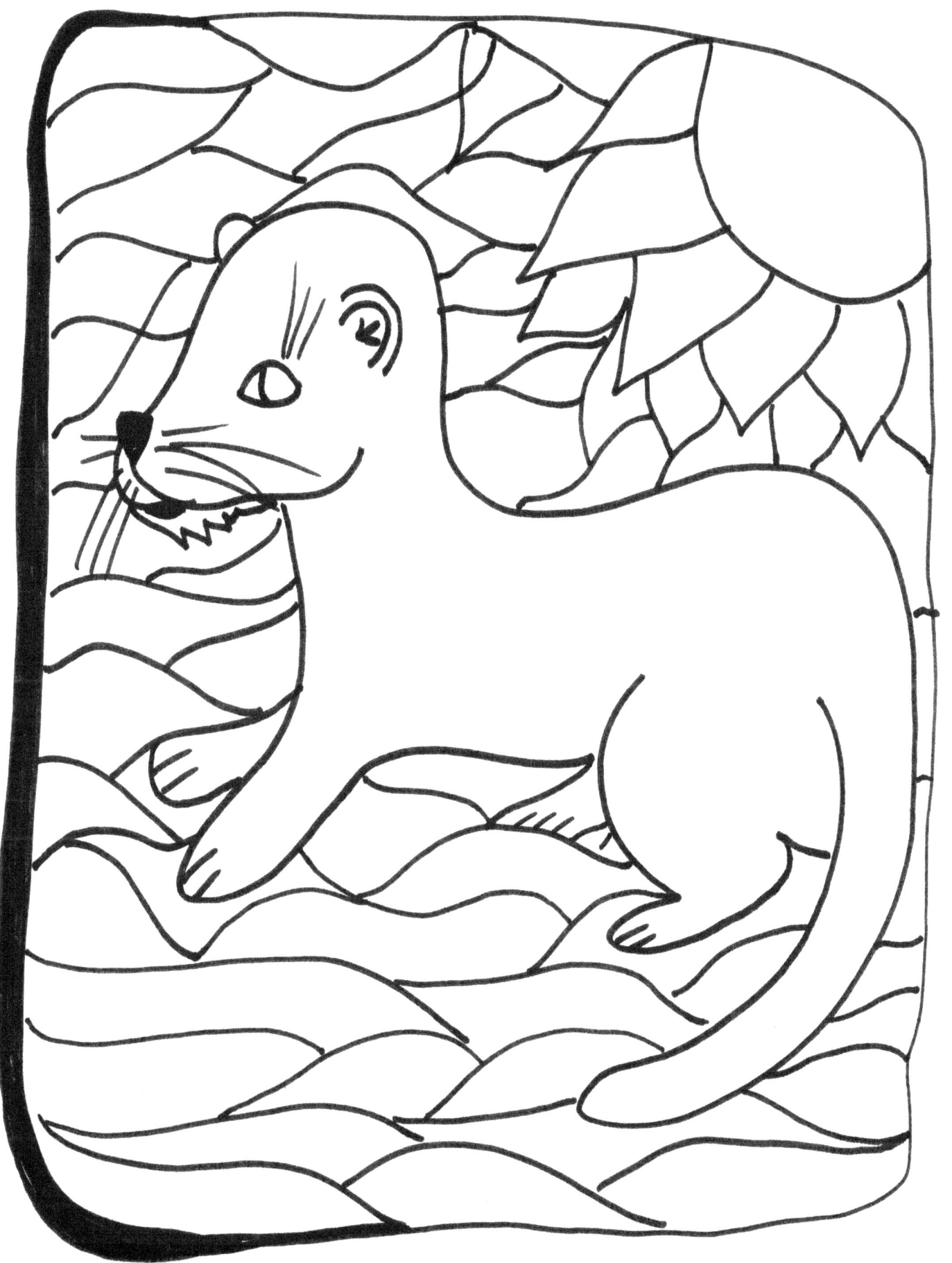

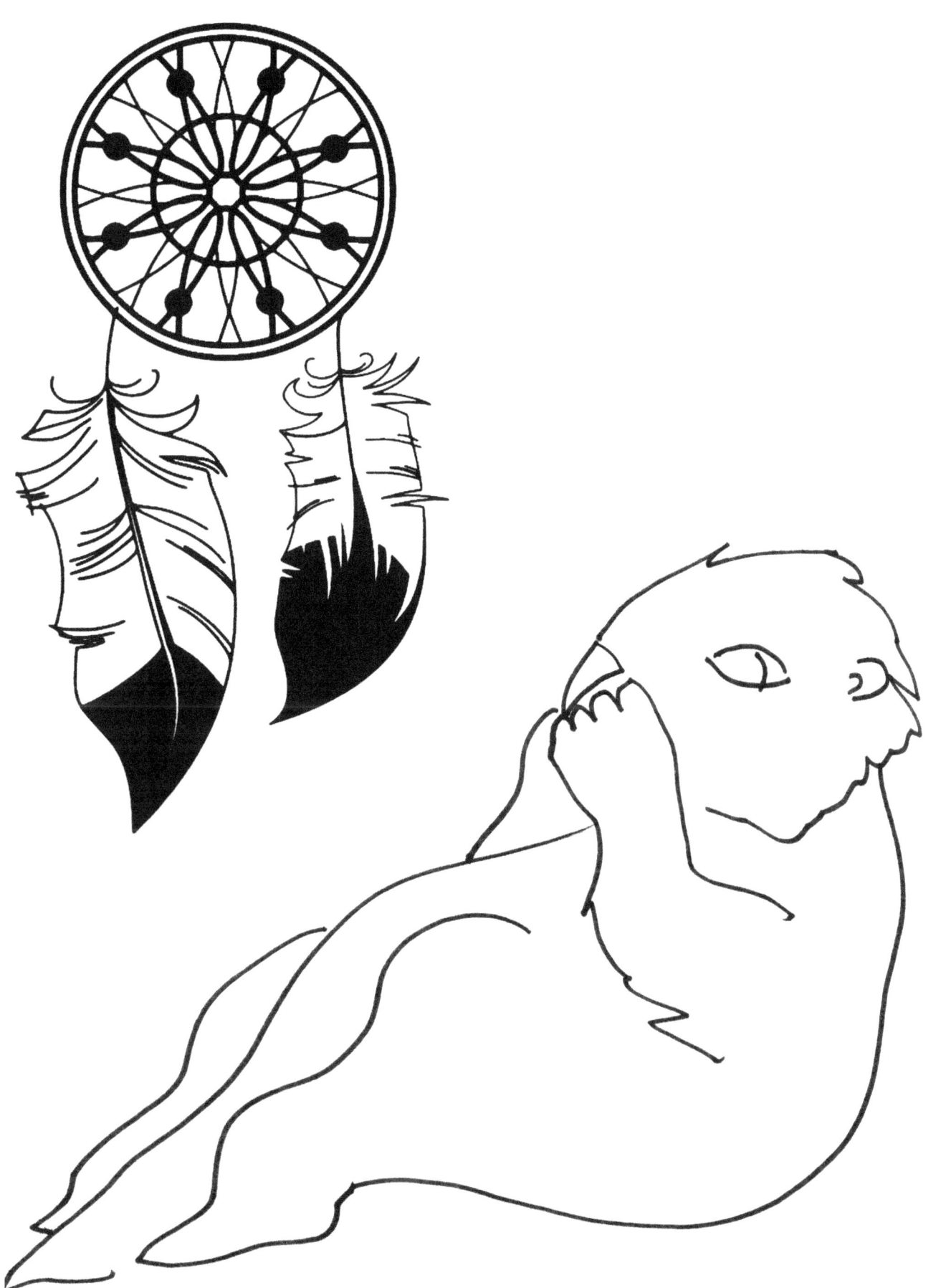

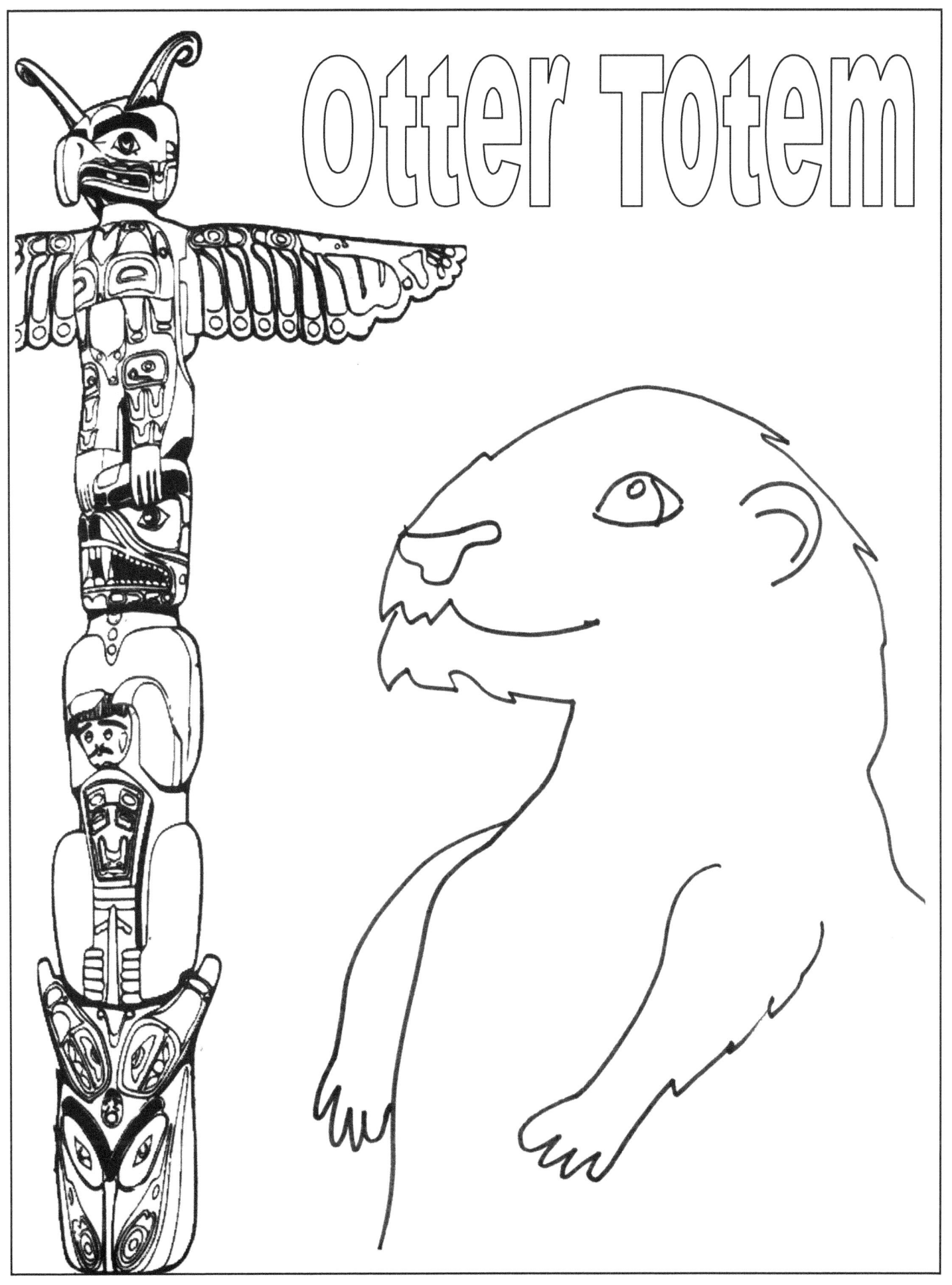

Otter Totem

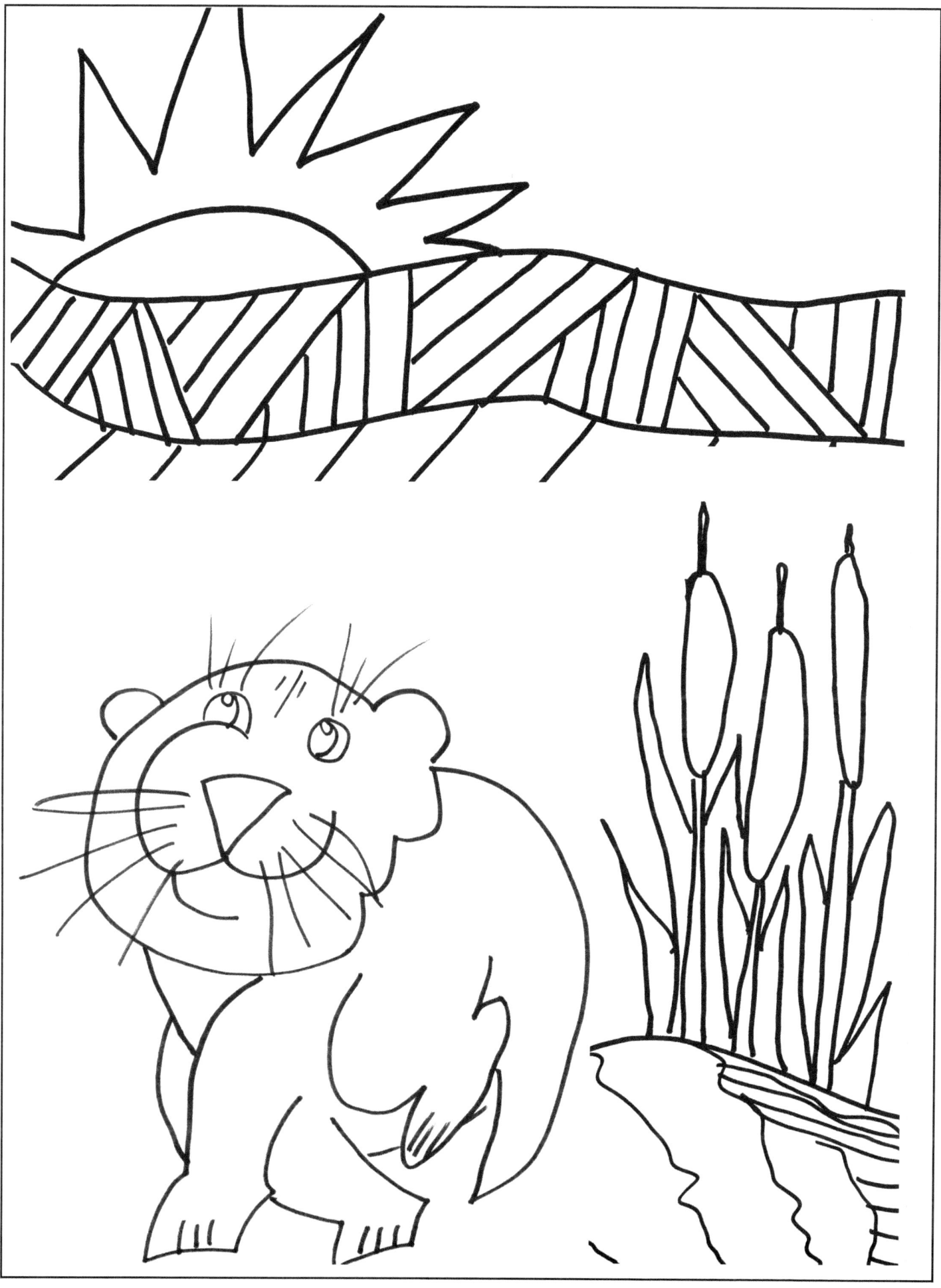

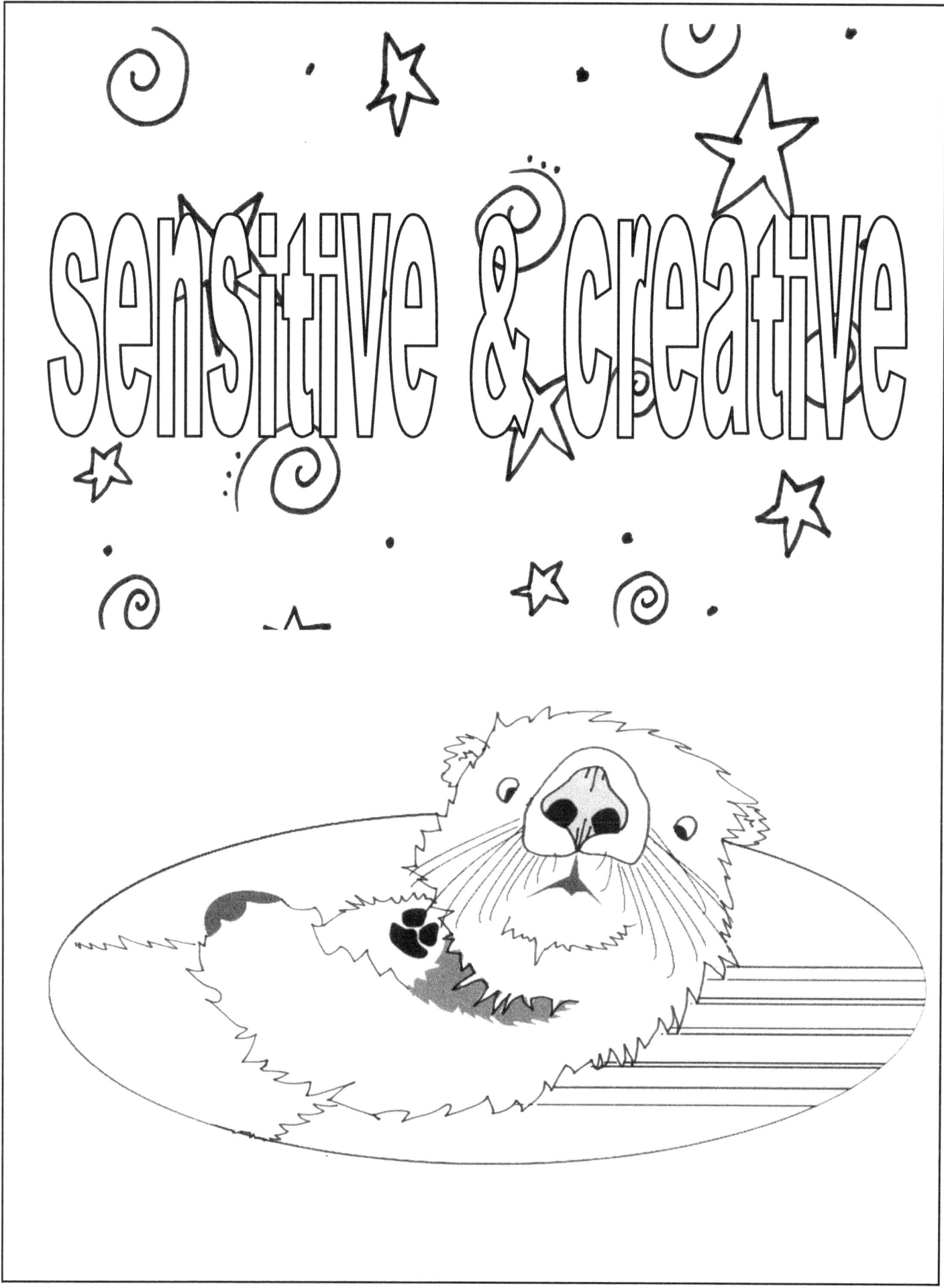

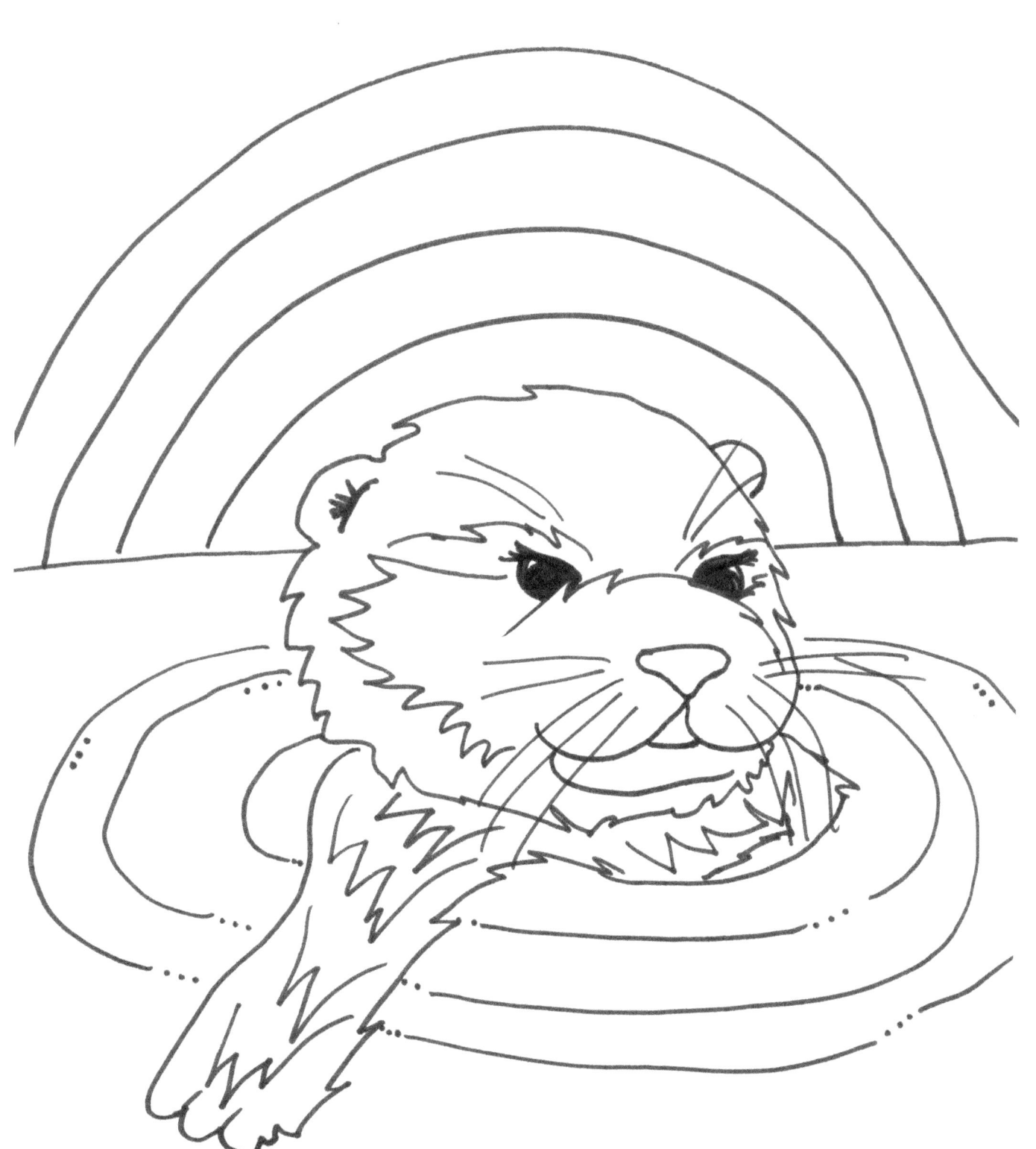

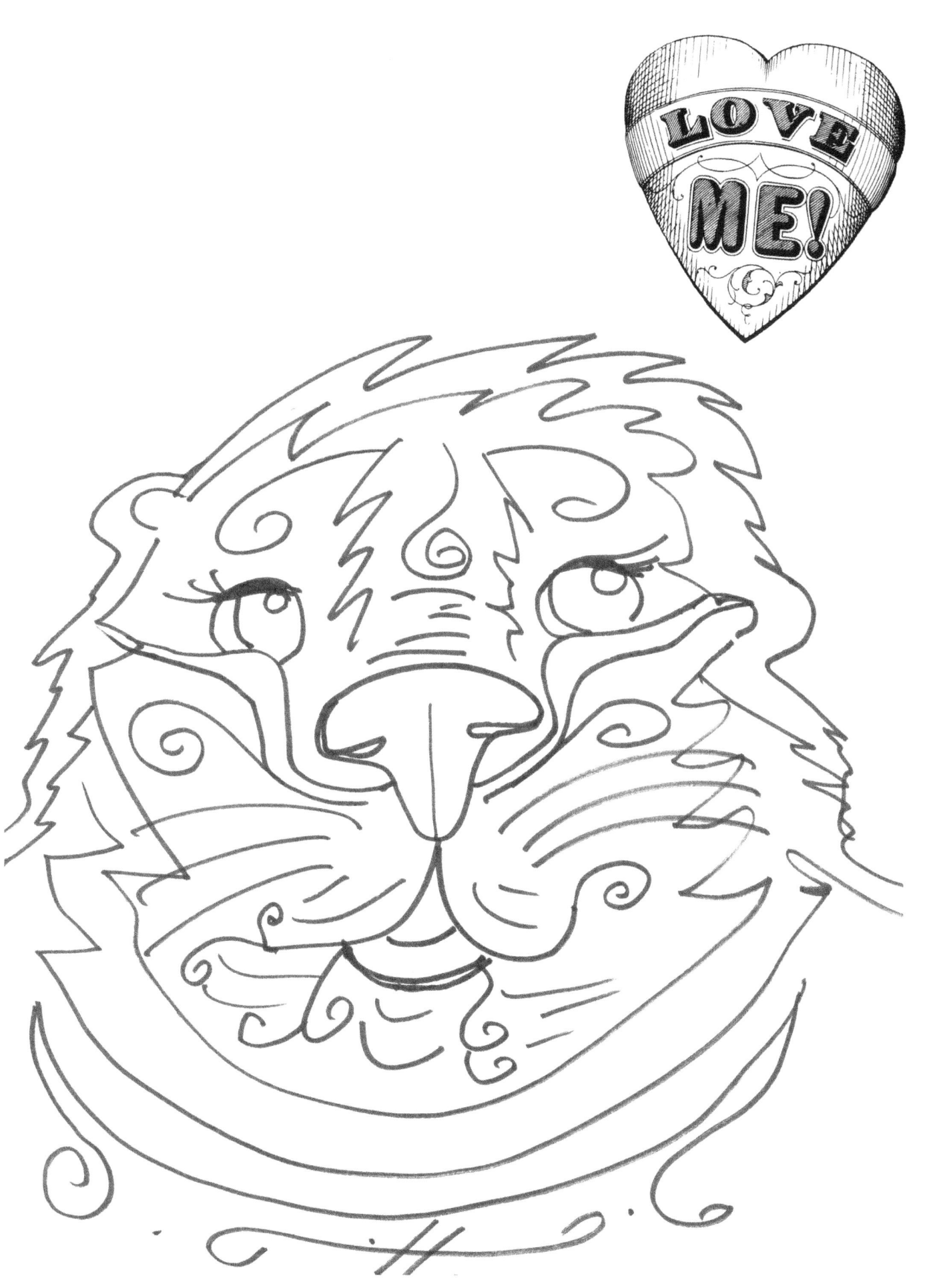

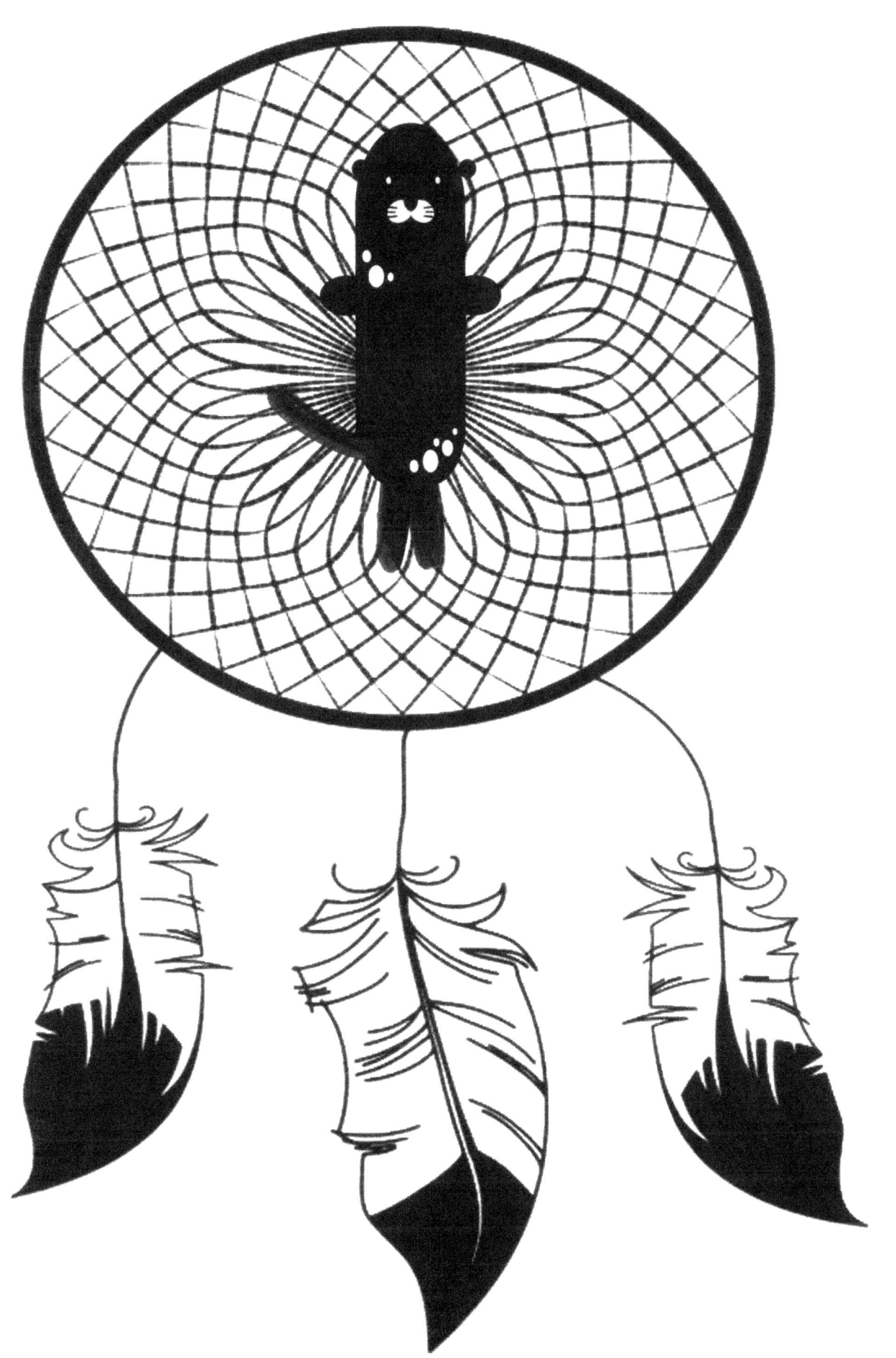

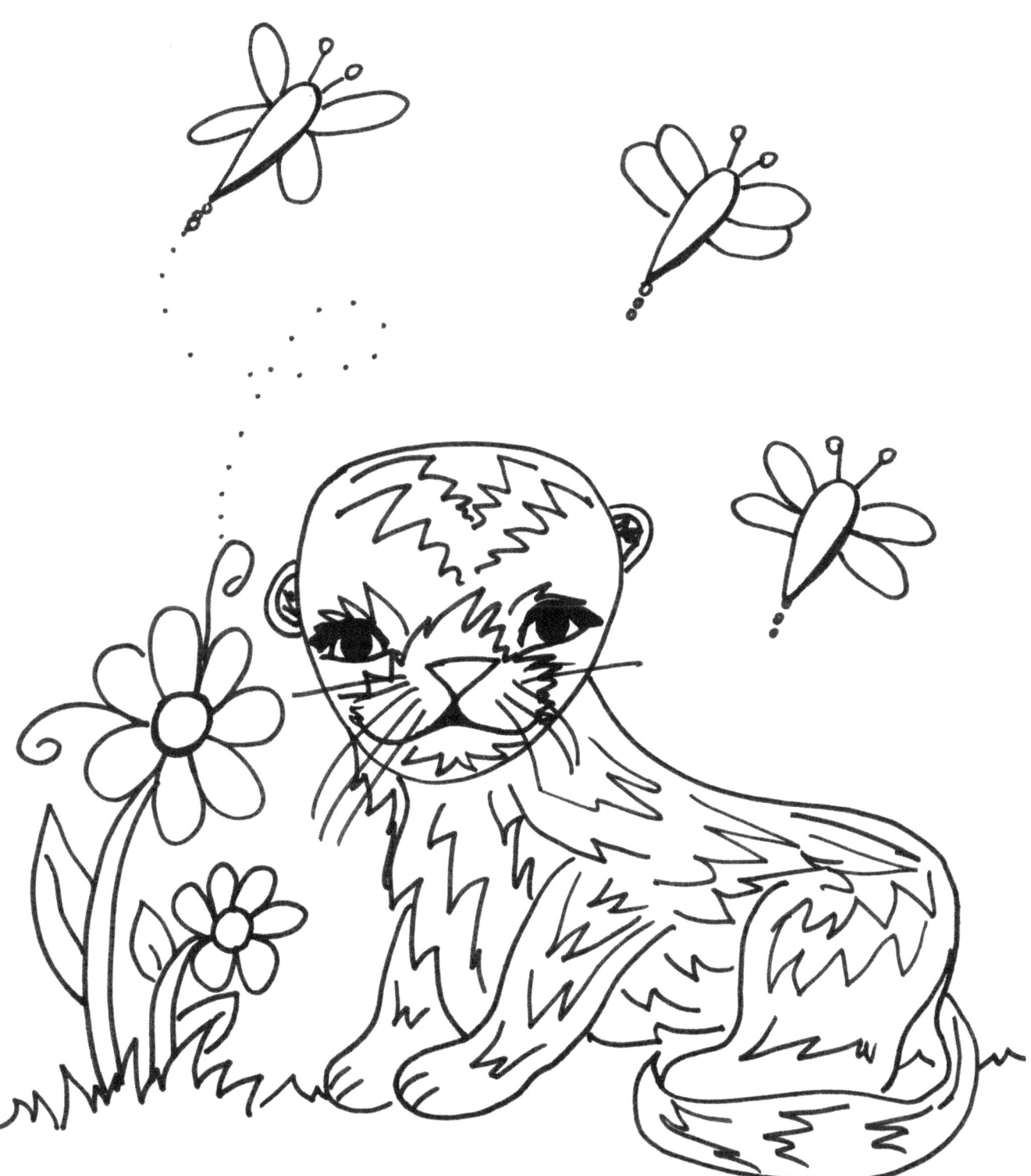

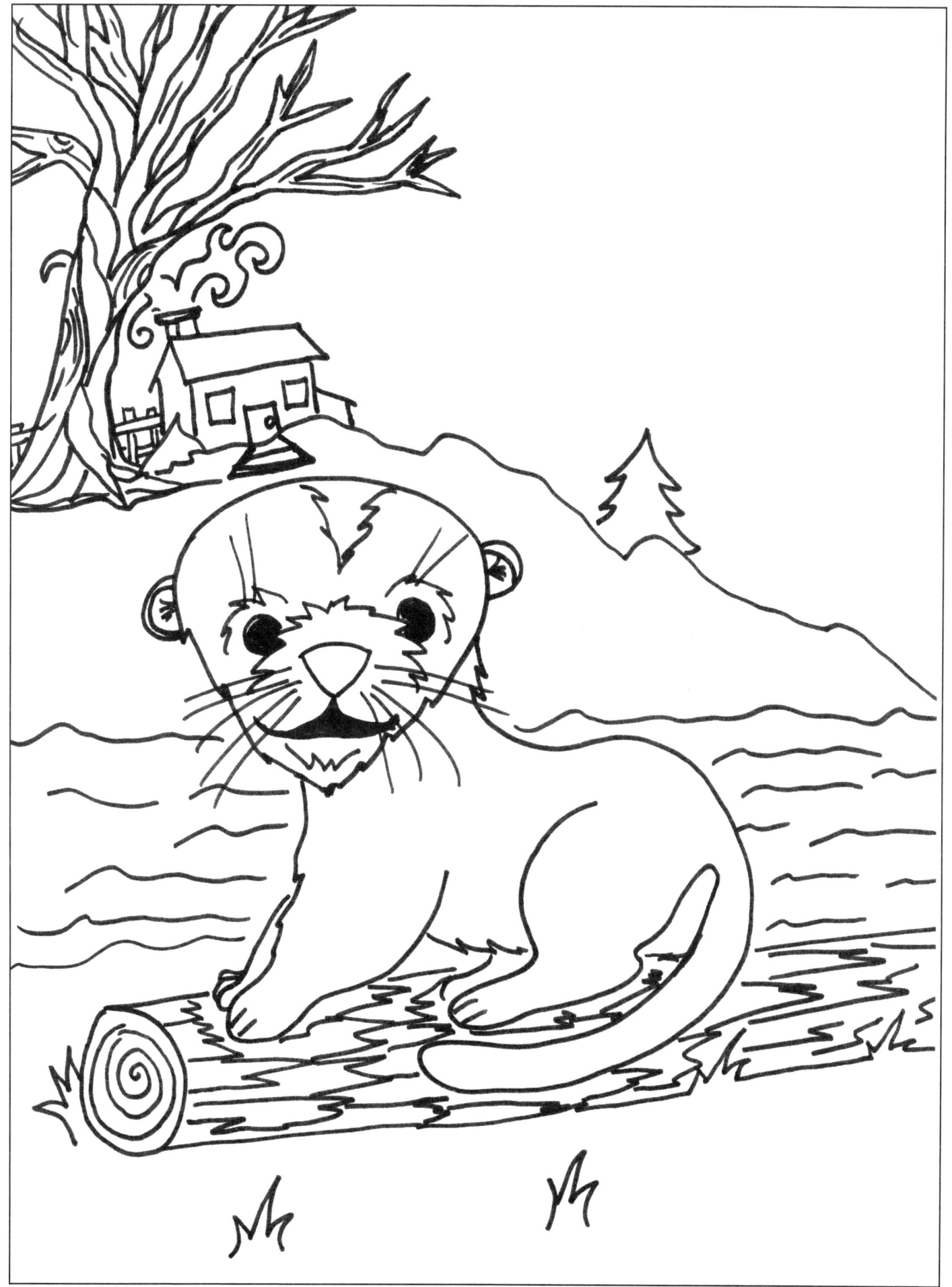

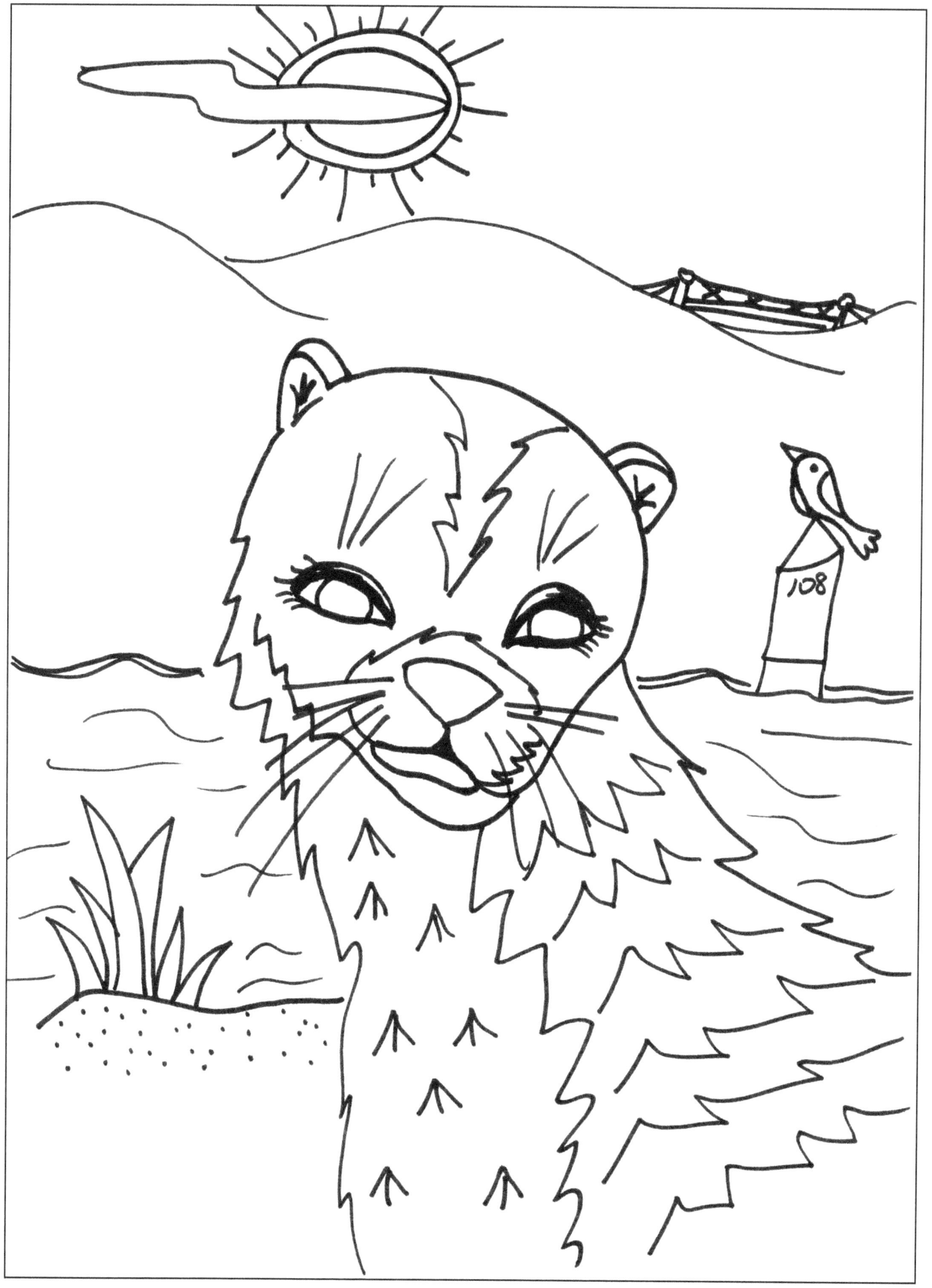

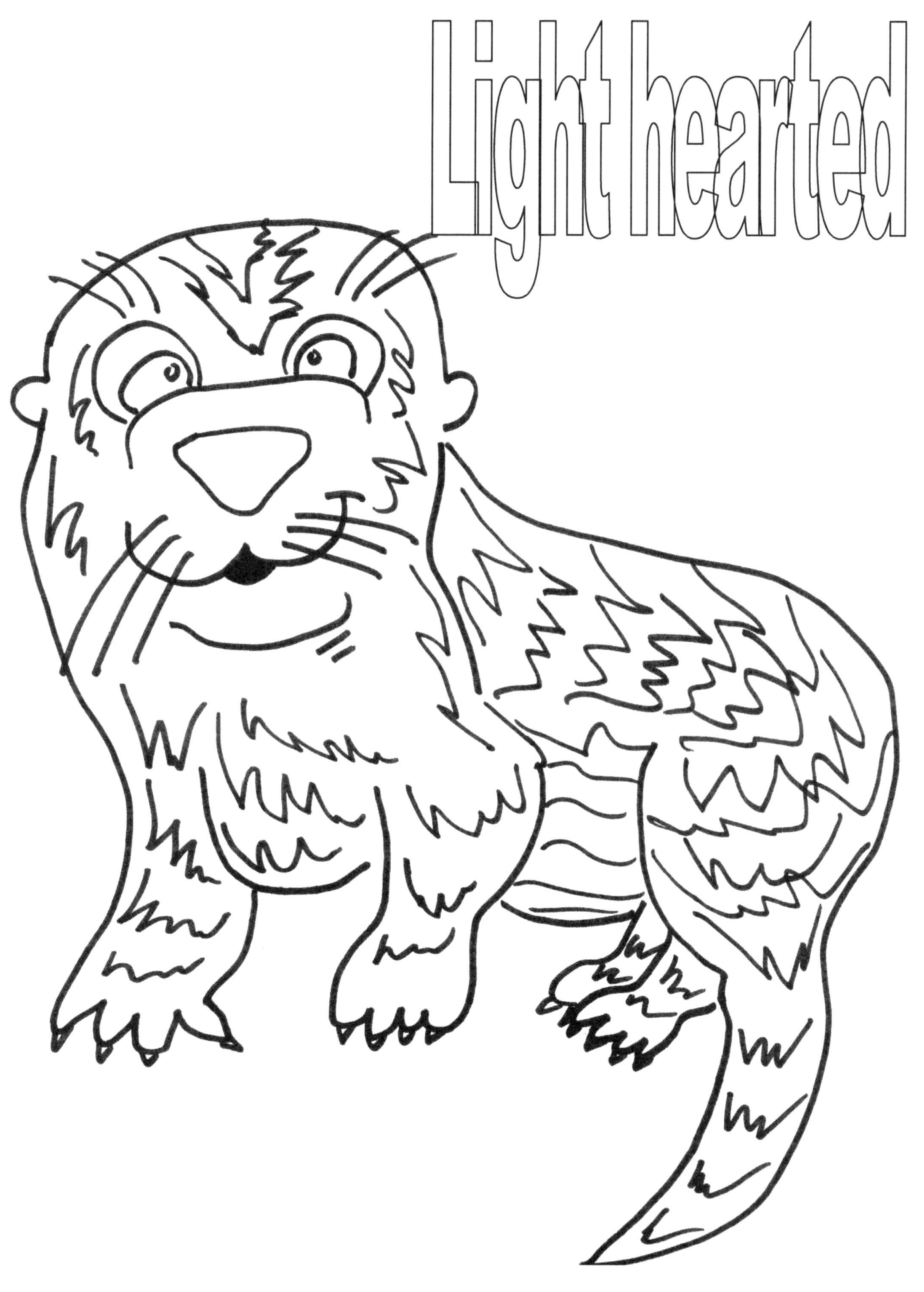

Light hearted

About the Creator:

Tammy Lawrence-Cymbalisty is an Alternative Care provider working in the Kitchener/Waterloo Region. Since 2001 she has helped many people find peace, happiness, harmony and further purpose in their lives.

Tammy holds many degrees including: B.A. Sociology (Trent University), Certified Yoga Teacher, Reiki Master/Teacher, HypnoBirthing® Practitioner, Meditation Teacher, Workshop facilitator, Writer, Personal Growth Coach.

She lives with her husband, two felines and a school of fins in Cambridge, ON

Find out more by following Tammy on social media:

http://www.twitter.com/tllc

http://www.tinyurl.com/tlcservices

May you find peace

May you find happiness

May you be free from suffering

Namaste, Tammy

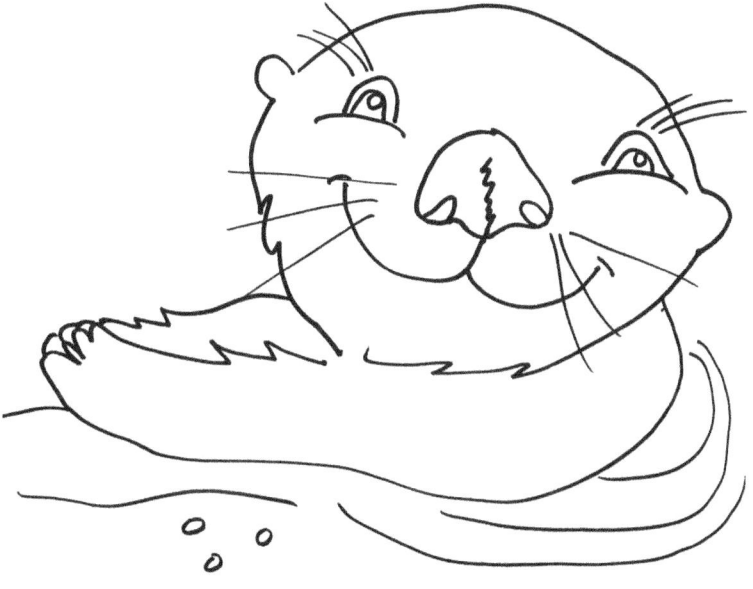

www.ingramcontent.com/pod-product-compliance
Lightning Source LLC
Chambersburg PA
CBHW080545190526

45169CB00007B/2637